Dedication: I want to dedicate this book to the men and women of public safety. We hold the best job in the world. As such, we are the ultimate recruiting team regardless of your department's recruiting efforts. If we don't get busy recruiting in our sphere of influence, we are going to face staffing shortages like you can not even imagine. So get busy recruiting.

INTRODUCTION

This book is the result of the intersection of two worlds. One World has over 20+ years of experience in the fire service. The other world is that of the owner and founder of a large digital marketing firm in Atlanta, GA. I live in both of those worlds.

Witnessing recruiting techniques that are designed by boomers to reach a Gen Z audience helped me to realize that my public safety family needs some help in this area.

The truth is that you just do not know what you do not know. This book is designed the solve that problem.

The staffing issue you are experiencing is just the beginning of what is going to be a catastrophic staffing shortage like you have never experienced in the past.

If you would like our help solving this very complex problem and you have the budget, we have experienced teams standing by to help.

You can engage with a fire-specific recruiting team at:

firerecruiting.co

And a police-specific recruiting team at :

policerecruiting.co

CONTENTS

IGNITE: A STRATEGIC GUIDE TO SOLVING FIRE & POLICE RECRUITING CHALLENGES WITH DIGITAL SOLUTIONS

PURPOSE AND STRUCTURE OF THE BOOK

This book aims to introduce the power of digital messaging to public safety. Also, it acts as a reference guide so that the reader can look up a topic and read the related chapter on how to utilize a specific digital tactic. This means that some of the content may seem duplicative if you are reading the book straight through. If you come across content that has already been stated, simply scan until you get to new content.

CHAPTER 1: UNDERSTANDING THE LANDSCAPE: CHALLENGES IN FIRE AND POLICE RECRUITING

Recruiting individuals to serve in fire and police departments is a critical aspect of maintaining public safety and security in communities. However, in recent years, fire and police recruiting efforts have faced a multitude of challenges that have made it increasingly difficult to attract qualified candidates. In this chapter, we will delve into the current landscape of fire and police recruitment, exploring the various hurdles that departments encounter and the implications these challenges have for the future of public safety.

Shortage of Qualified Applicants

One of the primary challenges facing fire and police

departments is the shortage of qualified applicants. Despite the importance of these roles in safeguarding communities, many departments struggle to attract individuals with the necessary skills, qualifications, and dedication to serve in these demanding professions. The reasons behind this shortage are multifaceted.

Firstly, low unemployment rates in many regions have reduced the pool of available candidates seeking employment, making it more challenging for departments to find suitable recruits. Additionally, competition from other industries that offer potentially higher salaries, better benefits, and less risky working environments can dissuade individuals from pursuing careers in fire and police services. Moreover, changing societal attitudes towards public service careers have led to a decline in interest among younger generations, further exacerbating the shortage of qualified applicants.

Aging Workforce

Another significant challenge confronting fire and police departments is the aging workforce. Many current personnel within these departments are approaching retirement age, leading to an impending wave of retirements that will leave vacancies to be filled. The loss of experienced and seasoned professionals poses a considerable challenge for departments, as we must find ways to recruit and train new talent to fill these critical roles. Moreover, the departure of veteran officers and firefighters can result in a loss of institutional knowledge and expertise, further compounding the challenge of maintaining operational effectiveness.

Diversity and Inclusion

Achieving diversity and inclusion within fire and police departments remains an ongoing challenge. Despite efforts to promote diversity and equity, many departments struggle to recruit candidates from diverse backgrounds. The lack of diversity within these departments not only undermines their ability to reflect the communities they serve but also contributes to tensions and mistrust between law enforcement agencies and marginalized populations. Addressing this challenge requires proactive measures to attract and retain a more diverse workforce, including targeted recruitment strategies, outreach programs, and cultural competency training.

Negative Public Perception

Public perception plays a significant role in shaping attitudes towards careers in fire and police services. Unfortunately, negative media coverage, high-profile incidents of misconduct, and ongoing scrutiny of law enforcement agencies have contributed to a decline in public trust and confidence in these professions. As a result, many individuals may be deterred from pursuing careers in fire and police services due to concerns about safety, job satisfaction, and ethical considerations. Overcoming the stigma associated with these professions and rebuilding trust in the community is essential for revitalizing recruitment efforts and attracting qualified candidates. While it seems like a monumental task an adequately funded local branding campaign can shift this perception in your community and your potential labor pool.

Recruitment and Retention Costs

Recruiting and retaining qualified personnel come with significant financial costs for fire and police departments. The recruitment process, which includes advertising, testing, background checks, and training, can be resource-intensive and costly. Moreover, high turnover rates within these departments can further strain budgets, as departments must invest in ongoing recruitment efforts to fill vacancies created by attrition. Balancing the need to attract top talent with limited financial resources poses a considerable challenge for departments, necessitating creative and cost-effective recruitment strategies.

Technological Advancements and Skills Gap

Advancements in technology have transformed the landscape of modern policing and firefighting, requiring recruits to possess a diverse skill set that encompasses both traditional and emerging competencies. From proficiency in data analysis and digital forensics to knowledge of advanced equipment and tools, today's recruits must be prepared to navigate a rapidly evolving technological landscape. Bridging the gap between traditional policing and firefighting practices and emerging technologies presents a challenge for recruitment efforts, as departments seek candidates who can adapt to the demands of modern public safety roles.

Mental Health and Wellness

The demanding and high-stress nature of fire and police work can take a toll on the mental health and well-being of personnel. Exposure to traumatic incidents, long hours, and the pressure to perform under challenging circumstances can contribute to high rates of stress, burnout, and mental health disorders among firefighters and law enforcement officers. Addressing the mental health needs of personnel and providing adequate support systems is essential for recruitment and retention efforts, as individuals are more likely to pursue careers in professions that prioritize their well-being and offer resources for coping with job-related stressors.

The challenges facing fire and police recruiting efforts are complex and multifaceted, requiring thoughtful strategies and proactive solutions to overcome. From addressing shortages of qualified applicants to promoting diversity and inclusion within departments, there is no shortage of obstacles to navigate in the recruitment process. However, by understanding the digital landscape of fire and police recruitment and investing in these channels, departments can develop effective strategies to attract and retain the next generation of public safety professionals. In the chapters that follow, we will explore innovative approaches and best practices for overcoming these challenges and revitalizing recruitment efforts in the fire and police sectors.

CHAPTER 2: LEVERAGING DIGITAL MARKETING TECHNIQUES FOR FIRE AND POLICE RECRUITING

In an era dominated by digital technology and online communication, traditional recruitment methods alone will no longer suffice to address the complex challenges facing fire and police departments. Current digital marketing techniques offer innovative solutions to overcome recruitment hurdles and attract qualified candidates to public safety professions. We will explore the potential of digital marketing strategies to revolutionize fire and police recruiting efforts, offering insights into how departments can leverage these techniques to effectively reach and engage prospective recruits.

Demographic Targeting: Reaching the Right Candidates

Digital marketing enables fire and police departments to target their recruitment efforts with precision, reaching specific demographic groups most likely to be interested in public safety careers. By leveraging data analytics and online targeting tools, departments can identify and engage with potential recruits based on factors such as age, gender, location, education level, and interests. Targeted advertising campaigns can be tailored to resonate with different demographic segments, ensuring that recruitment messages are relevant and compelling to diverse audiences. By focusing their resources on reaching the right candidates, departments can maximize the effectiveness of their recruitment efforts and attract individuals who are well-suited to the demands of the fire and police professions. The last thing we need is churn.

Messaging: Crafting Compelling Narratives

Messaging principles offer a powerful framework for shaping recruitment messages that resonate with prospective recruits. By framing recruitment efforts within a compelling narrative that highlights the purpose, values, and impact of fire and police work, departments can capture the attention and imagination of potential candidates. Storytelling techniques can be used to showcase real-life examples of the meaningful contributions that firefighters and law enforcement officers make to their communities, inspiring individuals to consider careers in public safety. By conveying a clear and compelling message about the importance and rewards of serving in fire and police departments, departments can attract candidates who are motivated by a sense of purpose and commitment to public service.

Search Ads: Increasing Visibility and Reach

Search engine advertising offers an effective way for fire and police departments to increase their visibility and reach among potential recruits. By bidding on relevant keywords and targeting specific geographic areas, departments can ensure that their recruitment ads appear prominently on search engine results pages when individuals are actively searching for information about public safety careers. Search ads can be tailored to align with specific recruitment objectives, such as promoting job openings, highlighting recruitment events, or driving traffic to department websites. By strategically optimizing ad content and targeting parameters, departments can maximize the effectiveness of their search advertising campaigns and connect with qualified candidates who are actively seeking opportunities in fire and police services.

Social Media Paid Ads: Engaging with Prospective Recruits

Many social media users do not know that these platforms throttle unpaid messaging. If your department is only posting content to your social media channels, you are severely limiting your reach. When you consider who your target market is, you are effectively wasting your time. Social media paid advertising offers a dynamic platform for fire and police departments to engage with prospective recruits and showcase the opportunities available in public safety careers. By leveraging the targeting capabilities of social media platforms, departments can reach specific demographic groups, interests, and behaviors, ensuring that their recruitment messages are seen by individuals who are most likely to be interested in fire and police professions. Social media paid ads can be used to promote recruitment events, share success stories from current personnel, and highlight the benefits of working in fire and police departments. By fostering meaningful interactions and dialogue with potential recruits on social media, departments can build relationships, generate interest, and ultimately, attract qualified candidates to join their ranks.

Programmatic Advertising: Streamlining Recruitment Efforts

Programmatic advertising offers a streamlined and data-driven approach to recruiting that enables fire and police departments to efficiently reach and engage prospective candidates across multiple online channels. By utilizing automated ad buying platforms and real-time bidding algorithms, departments can target their recruitment ads with precision, optimizing placement, timing, and messaging to maximize effectiveness. Programmatic advertising offers a scalable solution for departments of all sizes, allowing them to allocate resources strategically and adapt their recruitment strategies based on performance metrics and insights. By harnessing the power of programmatic advertising, departments can streamline their recruitment efforts, increase efficiency, and attract qualified candidates to fill critical roles in fire and police services.

IP Targeting: Personalizing Recruitment Messages

IP targeting technology enables fire and police departments to deliver personalized recruitment messages to individuals based on their geographic location. By mapping IP addresses to specific households or organizations, departments can target their ads to reach individuals in local communities, educational institutions, military bases, and other relevant locations. IP-targeted ads can be tailored to align with local recruitment initiatives, such as promoting career fairs, open houses, or recruitment seminars. By delivering relevant and timely recruitment messages directly to individuals within their communities, departments can increase awareness, drive engagement, and generate interest in fire and police careers among residents.

Landing Pages: Optimizing the Recruitment Experience

Landing pages play a critical role in the recruitment process, serving as the gateway for prospective candidates to learn more about fire and police careers and take action. By creating dedicated landing pages that are optimized for conversion, departments can provide visitors with valuable information about job opportunities, requirements, benefits, and application processes. Landing pages can be designed to align with specific recruitment campaigns, offering tailored messaging and call to action that prompt visitors to take the next step in the recruitment process. By optimizing landing pages for user experience, responsiveness, and accessibility, departments can enhance the recruitment experience, streamline the application process, and increase the likelihood of attracting qualified candidates to join their teams.

Data Analytics: Measuring and Optimizing Recruitment Performance

Data analytics offer valuable insights into the effectiveness of fire and police recruitment efforts, enabling departments to measure, analyze, and optimize performance metrics in real time. By tracking key performance indicators such as website traffic, ad engagement, conversion rates, and applicant demographics, departments can gain a deeper understanding of the effectiveness of their digital marketing campaigns and identify areas for improvement. Data analytics tools and dashboards provide departments with actionable insights that inform strategic decision-making, allowing them to allocate resources efficiently, refine targeting parameters, and optimize messaging to enhance recruitment outcomes. By leveraging data analytics to continuously monitor and refine their recruitment strategies, departments can maximize their impact, attract top talent, and build a pipeline of qualified candidates for fire and police positions.

Digital marketing techniques offer powerful tools and strategies for fire and police departments to overcome the challenges of recruiting in today's competitive landscape. By leveraging demographic targeting, effective messaging, search ads, social media ads, programmatic advertising, IP targeting, landing pages, and data analytics, departments can effectively reach and engage prospective recruits, increase awareness of fire and police careers, and attract qualified candidates to join their ranks. By embracing digital marketing as a cornerstone of their recruitment efforts, departments can position themselves for success in recruiting the next generation of public safety professionals.

CHAPTER 3: UNDERSTANDING GENERATIONAL DIFFERENCES: KEY DEMOGRAPHICS FOR NEW EMPLOYEE RECRUITMENT

In today's diverse workforce, understanding the unique characteristics and preferences of different generations is essential for effective employee recruitment and retention. From Baby Boomers to Generation Z, each generation brings its values, expectations, and communication styles to the workplace. In this chapter, we will explore the distinct characteristics of each generation and identify key demographics that public safety agencies can target in their recruitment efforts. At first glance, it would appear that only targeting Generation Z or millennial demographics would be the most efficient. We must remember that every Gen Z or millennial most likely has Gen X and Boomer parents and grandparents that have a large influence on life decisions.

The Silent Generation (Born 1928-1945)

The Silent Generation, also known as the Traditionalists, grew up during times of economic hardship and war. They value loyalty, stability, and respect for authority. While many members of this generation have already retired, some may still be active in the workforce, bringing decades of experience and wisdom to their roles.

Baby Boomers (Born 1946-1964)

Baby Boomers are known for their strong work ethic, ambition, and dedication to their careers. They value stability, financial security, and opportunities for advancement. Many Baby Boomers are nearing retirement age, but some may choose to continue working or pursue second careers in public safety.

Generation X (Born 1965-1980)

Generation X, often referred to as the "Latchkey Generation," grew up during a time of social and economic change. They value independence, work-life balance, and flexibility in their careers. Generation Xers are known for their entrepreneurial spirit and willingness to challenge traditional norms.

Millennials (Born 1981-1996)

Millennials, also known as Generation Y, are the largest generation in the workforce today. They are tech-savvy, socially conscious, and value-driven. Millennials prioritize work-life balance, career growth, and opportunities to make a positive impact in their communities. Countless millennials are looking for a different career right now. Public safety agencies targeting this demographic should highlight the meaningful and rewarding nature of public service careers, opportunities for professional development, and the use of technology and innovation in their recruitment efforts.

Generation Z (Born 1997-2012)

Generation Z, the youngest generation to enter the workforce, is known for its digital native status and entrepreneurial mindset. They value authenticity, diversity, and social responsibility. Generation Z'ers seek meaningful work that aligns with their values and offers opportunities for creativity and self-expression. Gen Z is also less confident and will question their ability to be successful in public safety careers. Public safety agencies recruiting from this demographic should emphasize the importance of public service, the opportunity to make a difference in their communities, reinforce training and preparation for success, and the use of technology and innovation in their recruitment efforts.

Shaped by the digital age and coming of age during times of social and economic change, Gen Z exhibits distinct characteristics and preferences that set them apart from previous generations. We will explore the demographics of Generation Z, examining their diversity, values, attitudes, and behaviors, and their implications for recruitment and engagement strategies in the workplace.

Demographic Profile

Age Distribution: Generation Z comprises individuals born between 1997 and 2012, making them primarily teenagers and young adults in their late teens to mid-20s.

Diversity: Generation Z is the most racially and ethnically

diverse generation in history. They are more likely to come from multicultural backgrounds, with a significant percentage identifying as non-white or biracial.

Digital Natives: Gen Z is the first generation to grow up entirely in the digital age, surrounded by technology from a young age. They are highly proficient in using smartphones, social media, and other digital platforms for communication, entertainment, and information.

Education: Many members of Generation Z are currently enrolled in higher education institutions, pursuing degrees in a wide range of fields. They value education and lifelong learning as pathways to personal and professional success.

Global Perspective: Generation Z is more globally connected than any previous generation, thanks to the internet and social media. They are exposed to diverse cultures, perspectives, and issues from around the world, shaping their worldview and social consciousness.

Characteristics and Values

Diversity and Inclusion: Generation Z values diversity and inclusion, advocating for equality and social justice. They are more likely to embrace diversity in all its forms and seek out inclusive environments where they feel accepted and respected.

Individuality and Authenticity: Gen Z'ers prioritize authenticity and individuality, preferring brands, organizations, and individuals that are genuine and transparent. They value personal expression and creativity and are drawn to brands that align with their values and beliefs.

Socially Conscious: Generation Z is socially conscious and environmentally aware, actively engaging in social and environmental activism. They are passionate about making a positive impact in their communities and the world at large, advocating for causes they believe in, and supporting brands and organizations that share their values.

Entrepreneurial Spirit: Many members of Generation Z exhibit an entrepreneurial mindset, seeking opportunities to innovate and create their paths to success. They are more likely to pursue entrepreneurship and freelancing as alternative career paths, leveraging their creativity and digital skills to pursue their passions.

Digital Fluency: Generation Z is highly fluent in digital technology, using smartphones, social media, and other digital platforms seamlessly in their daily lives. They are adept at navigating online spaces, consuming and creating digital content, and leveraging technology for communication, collaboration, and learning. They are looking to join employers who also embrace this technology. Your old-school recruiting efforts may be telling them all they need to know about your organization.

Implications for Recruitment and Engagement

Recruitment Strategies: To attract and engage Generation Z talent, organizations need to tailor their recruitment strategies to align with their values and preferences. This includes emphasizing diversity and inclusion initiatives, highlighting opportunities for personal and professional growth, and showcasing the organization's commitment to social responsibility and environmental sustainability.

Employer Branding: Building a strong employer brand is crucial for attracting and retaining Generation Z talent. Organizations should focus on showcasing their unique culture, values, and opportunities for growth and development, while also leveraging digital channels and social media platforms to reach and engage potential candidates.

Flexible Work Arrangements: Generation Z values flexibility in their work arrangements, including remote work options, flexible schedules, and opportunities for work-life balance. Organizations should highlight flexible work schedules such as 24/48, to accommodate the preferences of Gen Z employees and enhance their engagement and productivity.

Digital Engagement: Leveraging digital channels and technology is essential for engaging Generation Z employees. Organizations should invest in digital communication tools, collaboration platforms, and online learning resources to facilitate communication, collaboration, and professional development among Gen Z employees. If your computer system, software, or technology is out of date at your department it is most likely affecting your Gen Z recruitment and increasing your ghost rate (when candidates just do not show up for scheduled new hire onboarding events).

Purpose-Driven Work: Generation Z is motivated by purpose and values-driven work. Organizations should emphasize the meaningful impact of their work and the opportunity to contribute to positive change in society as key selling points in their recruitment efforts.

Understanding the unique characteristics and preferences of different generations is essential for public safety agencies to effectively recruit and retain top talent. By identifying key demographics within each generation, agencies can tailor their recruitment efforts to appeal to the values, aspirations, and expectations of potential candidates. Whether targeting Baby Boomers seeking a second career, Generation Xers looking for work-life balance, Millennials searching for meaningful work, or Generation Z'ers eager to make an impact, public safety agencies can leverage this knowledge to attract diverse talent and build strong and resilient teams.

CHAPTER 4: LEVERAGING DATA ANALYTICS TO UNDERSTAND GENERATION Z AUDIENCE BEHAVIOR AND PREFERENCES

In today's digital age, data analytics plays a crucial role in understanding consumer behavior, preferences, and trends. For organizations seeking to engage Generation Z, harnessing the power of data analytics is essential for gaining insights into the unique characteristics and preferences of this demographic cohort. In this chapter, we will explore how data analytics can be used to analyze the audience behavior and preferences of Generation Z, offering strategies and techniques for leveraging data to inform marketing, recruitment, and engagement efforts targeting this generation.

Understanding Generation Z: A Digital Native Generation

Digital Consumption Habits: Generation Z, born between 1997 and 2012, is the first generation to grow up entirely in the digital age. They are digital natives, with a high level of proficiency in using smartphones, social media, and other digital platforms for communication, entertainment, and information.

Multichannel Engagement: Gen Z'ers are active users of multiple digital channels, including social media platforms, streaming services, and online communities. They consume content across a variety of devices and platforms, often simultaneously, making them a highly engaged and digitally connected audience. Reaching this audience requires an omnichannel approach.

Preference for Visual Content: Generation Z gravitates towards visual content, such as videos, images, and infographics, over text based content. They prefer bite-sized, visually appealing content that is easy to consume and share across social media platforms.

Social Media Influence: Social media plays a central role in the lives of Generation Z, shaping their preferences, behaviors, and purchasing decisions. They rely on social media platforms such as Instagram, TikTok, and Snapchat to connect with peers, discover new trends, and engage with brands and content creators. Many Gen Z'ers report TikTok as their source of local and international news.

Leveraging Data Analytics to Understand Generation Z

Social Listening: Social listening involves monitoring and analyzing conversations and mentions of relevant topics, keywords, and hashtags on social media platforms. By tracking conversations related to specific topics or brands, organizations can gain insights into the interests, preferences, and sentiments of Generation Z.

Audience Segmentation: Audience segmentation involves dividing a target audience into distinct groups based on shared characteristics, interests, and behaviors. By segmenting Generation Z audiences based on demographic, psychographic, and behavioral factors, organizations can tailor their marketing messages and content to resonate with different segments.

Website Analytics: Website analytics tools, such as Google Analytics, provide valuable insights into the behavior and preferences of visitors to a website. By analyzing metrics such as page views, bounce rates, and time spent on a page, organizations can gain insights into which content resonates most with Generation Z visitors and optimize their websites accordingly.

Content Engagement Metrics: Content engagement metrics, such as likes, shares, comments, and click-through rates, provide insights into the effectiveness of content in capturing the attention and engagement of Generation Z audiences. By tracking these metrics across different digital channels and content types, organizations can identify trends and preferences among Gen Z'ers and refine their content strategies accordingly.

A/B Testing: A/B testing involves comparing two versions of a marketing asset or campaign to determine which performs better in terms of engagement, conversion, or other key metrics. By conducting A/B tests on marketing emails, social media ads, website landing pages, and other digital assets, organizations can identify the most effective strategies for engaging Generation Z audiences and optimize their campaigns accordingly.

Applying Data Insights to Marketing and Engagement Strategies

<u>Personalized Marketing:</u> Data analytics enables organizations to personalize marketing messages and content to resonate with the preferences and interests of Generation Z audiences. By leveraging data insights to tailor content, offers, and recommendations to individual preferences, organizations can increase engagement and conversion rates among Gen Z'ers.

<u>Influencer Marketing:</u> Influencer marketing involves partnering with social media influencers and content creators to promote products, services, or brands to their followers. By analyzing audience demographics, engagement metrics, and influencer partnerships, organizations can identify influencers who have a strong affinity with Generation Z audiences and leverage their influence to reach and engage this demographic effectively. Using influencers in "firefighter for a day" or police ride-along videos can help build your brand and trust factor.

<u>Content Strategy Optimization:</u> Data analytics enables organizations to optimize their content strategy based on insights into the preferences and behaviors of Generation Z audiences. By analyzing content engagement metrics, conducting A/B tests, and tracking trends in social media conversations, organizations can refine their content strategy to create more engaging and relevant content that resonates with Gen Z'ers.

<u>Cross-Channel Engagement:</u> Generation Z audiences engage with content across multiple digital channels and platforms.

By leveraging data analytics to track audience behavior and preferences across different channels, organizations can develop integrated, cross-channel engagement strategies that provide a cohesive and seamless experience for Gen Z'ers as they interact with brands and content.

Data analytics offers powerful insights into the behavior and preferences of Generation Z audiences, enabling organizations to create more targeted, personalized, and engaging marketing and engagement strategies. By leveraging data analytics tools and techniques to analyze social media conversations, segment audiences, track website analytics, measure content engagement, and conduct A/B testing, organizations can gain a deeper understanding of Generation Z and tailor their marketing and engagement efforts to effectively reach and engage this digitally savvy demographic.

Developing Generation Z Recruiting Personas for Effective Messaging in Recruiting

Recruiting Generation Z, the youngest cohort in the workforce, requires a nuanced understanding of their values, preferences, and aspirations. By developing recruiting personas that capture the diverse characteristics and motivations of Gen Z individuals, organizations can tailor their messaging and recruitment strategies to effectively attract and engage this demographic. Let's explore the process of developing Generation Z recruiting personas and discuss how to leverage these personas to create compelling and targeted messaging in recruiting efforts.

Understanding Generation Z: Key Characteristics and Preferences

Digital Natives: Generation Z is the first generation to grow up entirely in the digital age, surrounded by technology from a young age. They are highly proficient in using smartphones, social media, and other digital platforms for communication, entertainment, and information.

Diversity and Inclusion: Generation Z values diversity, equity, and inclusion, advocating for equality and social justice. They embrace diversity in all its forms and seek out inclusive environments where they feel accepted and respected.

Purpose-Driven: Gen Z'ers are motivated by purpose and values-driven work. They seek meaningful opportunities that allow them to make a positive impact in their communities and the world at large.

Authenticity: Generation Z prioritizes authenticity and transparency in their interactions with brands, organizations, and individuals. They are drawn to genuine, relatable messaging and are quick to identify and reject inauthentic or manipulative content.

Personalization: Gen Z'ers expect personalized experiences and communications tailored to their individual preferences and interests. They are more likely to engage with content and brands that offer personalized recommendations and recommendations.

Developing Generation Z Recruiting Personas

Conduct Research: Start by researching to gain insights into the characteristics, preferences, and behaviors of Generation Z. This may involve focus groups, interviews, and social listening to gather data on their values, interests, motivations, and aspirations.

<u>Identify Key Segments:</u> Based on the research findings, identify key segments or groups within Generation Z that share similar characteristics, values, and preferences. These segments may be based on factors such as demographic, psychographic, or behavioral characteristics.

<u>Create Persona Profiles:</u> Develop detailed persona profiles for each segment, outlining their demographics, interests, motivations, goals, challenges, and preferred communication channels. Include descriptive details and anecdotes to bring each persona to life and make them relatable to recruiters and hiring managers.

<u>Validate Personas:</u> Validate the personas with real Gen Z individuals through feedback sessions, surveys, or interviews. Ensure that the personas accurately reflect the needs, preferences, and aspirations of Generation Z and adjust them accordingly based on feedback.

<u>Finalize Personas:</u> Once validated, finalize the persona profiles, giving each persona a name, photo, and detailed description. These personas will serve as the foundation for developing targeted messaging and recruitment strategies tailored to the needs and preferences of Generation Z.

Crafting Messaging for Generation Z Recruiting Personas

<u>Understand Persona Preferences:</u> Tailor your messaging to resonate with the preferences and values of each persona. Consider factors such as language, tone, imagery, and content format to ensure that your messaging aligns with the preferences of Generation Z.

Highlight Purpose and Impact: Emphasize the meaningful and purpose-driven aspects of your organization and the opportunities it offers for making a positive impact in the world. Highlight initiatives, projects, or causes that resonate with the values and interests of each persona.

Be Authentic and Transparent: Authenticity is key to engaging Generation Z. Be genuine and transparent in your messaging, avoiding overly polished or salesy language. Use real stories, testimonials, and examples to demonstrate authenticity and build trust with Gen Z candidates.

Personalize Communication: Personalize your communication to each persona based on their interests, preferences, and motivations. Use targeted messaging and content that speaks directly to the needs and aspirations of each persona, demonstrating that you understand and value their individuality.

Use Visual and Interactive Content: Generation Z gravitates towards visual and interactive content that is engaging and shareable. Use videos, infographics, interactive quizzes, and other multimedia content to capture their attention and convey your message engagingly and memorably.

Implementing Persona-Based Recruiting Strategies

Tailor Recruitment Channels: Select recruitment channels and platforms that are preferred by each persona based on their communication preferences. This may include social media platforms, messaging apps, online communities, or niche job boards that align with the interests and preferences of each persona.

Customize Recruitment Events: Customize recruitment events, such as career fairs, information sessions, or campus visits, to appeal to the interests and preferences of each persona. Offer interactive activities, workshops, or presentations that cater to the specific needs and aspirations of each persona.

Engage Influencers and Ambassadors: Partner with influencers, brand ambassadors, or current employees who resonate with each persona to help amplify your messaging and reach a wider audience. Encourage them to share their experiences and insights with Gen Z candidates to build trust and credibility.

Measure and Iterate: Continuously measure the effectiveness of your persona-based recruiting strategies and messaging through metrics such as engagement rates, application conversion rates, and candidate feedback. Use this data to identify areas for improvement and iterate on your approach to better align with the needs and preferences of Generation Z.

Developing Generation Z recruiting personas provides organizations with valuable insights into the preferences, values, and aspirations of this demographic cohort, enabling them to create targeted and effective messaging in recruiting efforts. By conducting research, identifying key segments, creating persona profiles, and crafting personalized messaging, organizations can tailor their recruitment strategies to resonate with the needs and preferences of Generation Z.

CHAPTER 5: STORY-BASED MESSAGING PRINCIPLES IN FIRE & POLICE RECRUITMENT

In today's competitive job market, attracting top talent to fire and police departments requires more than just listing job requirements and benefits. It requires compelling storytelling that resonates with candidates on a deeper level. Story-based messaging principles offer a powerful technique for crafting recruitment messages that engage and inspire prospective recruits. In this chapter, we will explore the principles of story-based messaging and their application in recruitment messaging for fire and police departments.

Understanding story-based messaging

The Power of Storytelling: story-based messaging is based on the premise that storytelling is the most effective way to communicate a message and engage an audience. Stories have the power to capture attention, evoke emotions, and inspire action in ways that facts and data alone cannot. We are conditioned to consume story-based media. For example, almost every movie script follows the same pattern:

- A character has a problem
- They meet a guide
- The guide gives them a plan
- Success and failure are defined
- The character becomes the hero while almost succumbing to failure

In Star Wars, Harry Potter, Lord of the Rings, and Every Avenger Movie, the pattern is the same. We always relate to the hero. We picture ourselves as the hero. The mistake most commonly made in police and fire recruiting messaging is that we define the department as the hero. We talk about the department and what the department does, what the department pays, what benefits the department offers. To be effective the message needs to focus on the potential employee.

Make the recruit the hero and the department is simply the guide. What can the hero do when they join your department and you guide them to success? This is the message. Now frame that message using the demographic information we know about our target demographic Gen Z' ers and encompass their fears and their desires. What does success look like for them? What failures will you help them avoid?

Creating a Call to Action: Every recruitment message should include a clear call to action that prompts the audience to take the next step, whether it's applying for a job, attending an information session, or contacting the recruitment team for more information. The call to action should be specific, actionable, and easy to follow. You must tell them what to do next. If you just show a media without a specific and measurable call to action, your viewers will simply see it as poorly designed entertainment. This is why you hear quotes that most viewers will not watch a video longer than 30 seconds. The truth is they are quick to swipe if they feel the content does not apply to them.

Define the story early and provide a clear and measurable call to action.

Story-based messaging principles offer a powerful framework for crafting compelling recruitment messages that resonate with prospective recruits and inspire them to take action. By positioning the audience as the hero, highlighting their challenges and aspirations, and positioning the fire or police department as the guide that can help them achieve their goals, organizations can create messaging that engages, inspires, and motivates individuals to pursue careers in public safety.

CHAPTER 6: CRAFTING COMPELLING NARRATIVES FOR FIRE & POLICE RECRUITMENT

Recruiting top talent to fire and police departments requires more than just listing job requirements and benefits; it requires crafting compelling narratives that resonate with potential recruits on a personal level. By creating narratives that evoke emotion, highlight purpose, and showcase the impact of public safety careers, organizations can attract candidates who are passionate about serving their communities. In this chapter, we will explore strategies for crafting narratives that resonate with potential fire and police recruits and inspire them to join the ranks of first responders.

Understanding the Power of Narrative

Emotion and Connection: Narratives have the power to evoke

emotion and create a connection with the audience. By telling stories that resonate with the values, aspirations, and experiences of potential recruits, organizations can engage them on a deeper level and inspire them to take action.

Purpose and Meaning: Effective narratives highlight the purpose and meaning behind public safety careers, illustrating the importance of serving and protecting the community. By showcasing the impact that first responders have on people's lives, organizations can attract candidates who are motivated by a sense of purpose and fulfillment.

Authenticity and Relatability: Authenticity is key to crafting narratives that resonate with potential recruits. Stories should feel genuine, relatable, and reflective of the experiences of current first responders. By sharing real-life examples and testimonials, organizations can build trust and credibility with their audience.

Differentiation and Positioning: Narratives can also be used to differentiate the organization and position its team as the best. By highlighting unique features, benefits, and opportunities, organizations can attract candidates who align with their values and culture. Everyone wants to be on a winning team full of heroes.

Identifying Key Themes and Messages

Service and Sacrifice: One key theme in fire and police recruitment narratives is the idea of service and sacrifice. Stories should highlight the selflessness and bravery of first responders who put their lives on the line to protect others.

Community Impact: Narratives should also emphasize the

impact that first responders have on the community, from saving lives and preventing crime to building trust and fostering relationships with residents.

Career Development and Growth: Another important theme is career development and growth opportunities within the organization. Stories should showcase the training programs, advancement opportunities, and professional development resources available to recruits. Can they envision themselves as the future police chief or future fire chief who leads a team of heroes who make a difference every day.

Diversity and Inclusion: Organizations should also highlight their commitment to diversity and inclusion in their narratives. Stories should reflect the diversity of the department and showcase opportunities for all individuals to thrive and succeed. This is not your grandpa's police or fire department. Join the team that "gets it" and is working hard to make the world a better place.

Crafting Compelling Stories

Start with a Strong Hook: Begin by grabbing the audience's attention with a strong hook or opening statement that draws them into the story. This could be a compelling statistic, a powerful quote, or an intriguing question that piques their curiosity.

Create a Narrative Arc: Develop a narrative arc that follows a clear structure, including an introduction, rising action, climax, and resolution. Use storytelling techniques such as character development, conflict, and resolution to keep the audience engaged and invested in the story.

Use Vivid Imagery and Descriptive Language: Paint a vivid picture with descriptive language and imagery that helps the audience visualize the story. Use sensory details to create a sense of immersion and bring the narrative to life.

Include Real-Life Examples and Testimonials: Incorporate real-life examples and testimonials from current first responders to add authenticity and credibility to the narrative. Share stories of heroic acts, impactful experiences, and personal journeys that resonate with potential recruits.

Highlight the Why: Finally, make sure to communicate the why behind the narrative—why does this story matter, and what does it mean for potential recruits? Emphasize the purpose, meaning, and impact of public safety careers to inspire action and commitment.

Tailoring Narratives to Different Audiences

Recent High & College School Graduates: For recent graduates, narratives should emphasize the opportunities for growth, learning, and professional development within the organization. Highlight the training programs, mentorship opportunities, and career paths available to recruits.

Military Veterans: For military veterans, narratives should highlight the similarities between military service and public safety careers, such as teamwork, leadership, and a commitment to service. Showcase the transferable skills and experiences that veterans can bring to the role.

Career Changers: For individuals seeking a career change, narratives should focus on the opportunity to make a meaningful impact in a new field. Highlight the unique experiences, perspectives, and skills that career changers can bring to the organization.

Underrepresented Groups: Organizations should also tailor narratives to resonate with underrepresented groups, such as women and minorities. Highlight the diversity and inclusivity of the organization and showcase opportunities for all individuals to succeed.

Amplifying Narratives Through Multiple Channels

Social Media: Share narratives on social media platforms such as Facebook, Instagram, and Twitter to reach a wide audience and generate engagement. Use multimedia content such as videos, photos, and infographics to bring stories to life and make them shareable. Your department should invest heavily in becoming a media generation machine.

Website and Blog: Feature narratives on the organization's website and blog to provide potential recruits with more information and context. Create a dedicated section for recruitment stories and testimonials where visitors can learn more about the experiences of current first responders.

Recruitment Events: Incorporate narratives into recruitment events such as career fairs, information sessions, and open houses to engage potential recruits in person. Invite current first responders to share their stories and answer questions from attendees.

Community Outreach: Use narratives as part of community outreach efforts to build relationships with residents and stakeholders. Share stories through local media outlets, community organizations, and public events to raise awareness and interest in public safety careers.

Crafting compelling narratives is essential for attracting top talent to fire and police departments. By understanding the power of storytelling, identifying key themes and messages, and tailoring narratives to different audiences, organizations can create stories that resonate with potential recruits and inspire them to pursue careers in public safety. By amplifying narratives through multiple channels and engaging the community, organizations can build awareness, generate interest, and ultimately recruit the next generation of first responders.

CHAPTER 7: BUILDING TRUST AND AUTHENTICITY IN MESSAGING FOR FIRE & POLICE RECRUITING

In the competitive landscape of recruitment, building trust and authenticity in messaging is paramount for fire and police departments. Potential recruits seek organizations they can trust, where they feel valued, respected, and aligned with the organization's values and culture. In this chapter, we'll delve into strategies for cultivating trust and authenticity in recruitment messaging for fire and police departments, highlighting the importance of transparency, credibility, and genuine connection with prospective recruits.

The Importance of Trust and Authenticity in Recruitment

<u>Trust as a Foundation:</u> Trust serves as the foundation of any successful recruitment effort. Potential recruits are more likely to consider joining an organization they trust, where they believe their contributions will be valued and respected.

Authenticity as a Differentiator: Authenticity sets organizations apart in a crowded recruitment landscape. Authentic messaging resonates with potential recruits on a deeper level, fostering genuine connections and building long-term loyalty.

Impact on Recruitment Success: Building trust and authenticity in recruitment messaging directly impacts recruitment success. Organizations that prioritize transparency, honesty, and genuine engagement with potential recruits are more likely to attract top talent and retain employees over the long term.

Strategies for Building Trust and Authenticity in Messaging

Be Transparent and Honest: Transparency is key to building trust with potential recruits. Be honest about the opportunities, challenges, and expectations associated with working in the fire or police department. Avoid exaggerating benefits or downplaying potential drawbacks.

Showcase Real Stories and Testimonials: Authenticity is reinforced through real stories and testimonials from current employees. Share firsthand accounts of experiences, challenges, and successes within the organization to provide potential recruits with insight into what it's like to work there.

Highlight Organizational Values and Culture: Communicate the organization's values and culture authentically in recruitment messaging. Emphasize the importance of integrity, teamwork, respect, and service to the community, and showcase how these values are lived out by employees every day.

Foster Genuine Connections: Build genuine connections with

potential recruits by engaging in meaningful conversations and actively listening to their needs and concerns. Demonstrate empathy, understanding, and support for their aspirations and goals. Be available for questions and have adequate staff to quickly respond to texts, emails, or phone calls from potential recruits.

Provide Opportunities for Interaction: Offer opportunities for potential recruits to interact with current employees, leadership, and other stakeholders. This could include informational interviews, networking events, or shadowing opportunities that allow recruits to get a firsthand look at the organization's culture and values.

Leveraging Digital Platforms for Authentic Engagement

Use Social Media to Humanize the Organization: Social media platforms provide a powerful opportunity to humanize the organization and showcase its culture and values. Share behind-the-scenes glimpses of daily life in the fire or police department, highlight employee stories, and engage with followers authentically.

Encourage Employee Advocacy: Empower current employees to serve as brand ambassadors and advocates for the organization on social media. Encourage them to share their experiences, insights, and perspectives authentically, helping to build trust and credibility with potential recruits.

Respond Promptly and Transparently to Inquiries: Respond promptly and transparently to inquiries from potential recruits on digital platforms. Provide accurate and helpful information, address concerns or questions openly, and demonstrate a commitment to supporting and engaging with candidates throughout the recruitment process.

Showcase Diversity and Inclusion Efforts: Highlight the organization's commitment to diversity, equity, and inclusion in recruitment messaging on digital platforms. Showcase initiatives, programs, and employee resource groups that promote diversity and create an inclusive workplace culture.

Cultivating Authentic Leadership and Communication

Lead by Example: Authentic leadership is essential for building trust and credibility in recruitment messaging. Leaders should lead by example, demonstrating integrity, honesty, and empathy in their interactions with potential recruits and employees.

Communicate Openly and Honestly: Foster a culture of open and honest communication within the organization. Keep employees informed about relevant updates, changes, and initiatives, and encourage them to share feedback, ideas, and concerns openly.

Listen and Respond to Feedback: Actively listen to feedback from employees and potential recruits, and respond thoughtfully and transparently. Demonstrate a willingness to address concerns, make improvements, and adapt recruitment strategies based on feedback and insights.

Be Authentic in Your Branding and Messaging: Ensure that branding and messaging authentically reflect the organization's values, culture, and identity. Avoid using generic or cliché language and imagery, and instead strive for authenticity and resonance with potential recruits.

Building trust and authenticity in recruitment messaging is essential for attracting top talent to fire and police departments. By prioritizing transparency, honesty, and genuine engagement with potential recruits, organizations can build meaningful connections, foster trust, and inspire candidates to join their ranks as first responders. Through strategic use of digital platforms, cultivation of authentic leadership and communication, and development of compelling recruitment messaging, fire and police departments can effectively communicate their values, culture, and opportunities, and ultimately recruit the next generation of dedicated public safety professionals.

CHAPTER 8: THE IMPORTANCE OF SEARCH ENGINE OPTIMIZATION FOR POLICE AND FIRE RECRUITING WEBSITES

In the digital age, search engine optimization (SEO) plays a critical role in ensuring that police and fire recruiting websites are discoverable, visible, and accessible to potential recruits. With the majority of job seekers using search engines like Google to find employment opportunities, optimizing recruitment websites for search engines is essential for attracting top talent to police and fire departments. In this chapter, we will explore the importance of SEO for police and fire recruiting websites and discuss strategies for optimizing website content, improving search rankings, and attracting qualified candidates.

Understanding the Role of SEO in Recruitment

Visibility and Discoverability: SEO enhances the visibility and discoverability of police and fire recruiting websites by improving their rankings in search engine results pages (SERPs). Websites that appear higher in search results are more likely to be clicked on by job seekers, increasing their exposure to potential recruits.

Targeted Traffic: SEO helps attract targeted traffic to police and fire recruiting websites by ensuring that they appear in search results for relevant keywords and phrases. By optimizing website content for specific search terms related to public safety careers, organizations can attract qualified candidates who are actively seeking employment in the field.

Cost-Effective Marketing: SEO offers a cost-effective alternative to traditional advertising and marketing strategies for recruiting. Unlike paid advertising, which requires ongoing investment to maintain visibility, SEO generates organic traffic over time, providing a sustainable and cost-effective means of attracting recruits.

Long-Term Results: SEO produces long-term results that continue to benefit police and fire recruiting efforts over time. By consistently optimizing website content and adhering to SEO best practices, organizations can maintain and improve their search rankings, ensuring ongoing visibility to potential recruits.

Key Components of SEO for Police and Fire Recruiting Websites

Keyword Research: Keyword research is the foundation of SEO for police and fire recruiting websites. Identify relevant keywords and phrases that potential recruits are likely to use when searching for public safety careers, such as "police officer jobs" or "firefighter recruitment."

On-Page Optimization: On-page optimization involves optimizing website content, including headings, meta tags, and body copy, to align with targeted keywords and improve search rankings. Incorporate keywords naturally throughout website content while ensuring readability and relevance to the target audience.

Content Creation: Create high-quality, informative, and engaging content that addresses the needs and interests of potential recruits. Publish blog posts, articles, and resources that provide valuable insights into the recruitment process, career opportunities, training programs, and life as a first responder.

Website Structure and Navigation: Ensure that police and fire recruiting websites have a user-friendly structure and navigation that makes it easy for visitors to find information quickly and intuitively. Use descriptive URLs, clear headings, and internal linking to improve website usability and search engine visibility.

Mobile Optimization: With an increasing number of job seekers using mobile devices to search for employment opportunities, mobile optimization is essential for police and fire recruiting websites. Ensure that websites are mobile-friendly, with responsive design, fast loading times, and easy navigation on smartphones and tablets.

Local SEO for Police and Fire Departments

Google My Business: Claim and optimize your organization's

Google My Business listing to improve visibility in local search results. Provide accurate and up-to-date information, including location, contact details, hours of operation, and reviews from current and former employees.

Local Citations: Build local citations on relevant directories, review sites, and online communities to improve local search rankings for police and fire recruiting websites. Ensure that NAP (name, address, phone number) information is consistent across all citations to maximize visibility and credibility.

Geo-Targeted Keywords: Incorporate geo-targeted keywords into website content to improve visibility in local search results. Include location-specific terms such as city names, neighborhoods, or landmarks in page titles, headings, and meta descriptions to attract local recruits.

Location-Based Landing Pages: Create location-based landing pages for different recruitment regions or districts to target recruits in specific geographic areas. Customize landing page content to highlight local career opportunities, training programs, community partnerships, and benefits.

Measuring and Monitoring SEO Performance

Key Performance Indicators (KPIs): Define key performance indicators (KPIs) to track and measure the effectiveness of SEO efforts for police and fire recruiting websites. KPIs may include website traffic, search rankings, click-through rates, conversion rates, and applicant engagement metrics.

Web Analytics Tools: Use web analytics tools such as Google Analytics to monitor website traffic, user behavior, and conversion metrics. Track changes in website performance over time, identify areas for improvement and adjust SEO strategies accordingly to maximize recruitment outcomes.

SEO Audits and Assessments: Conduct regular SEO audits and assessments to identify technical issues, content gaps, and opportunities for optimization on police and fire recruiting websites. Address any issues promptly and implement recommendations to improve website performance and search rankings.

Search engine optimization is essential for police and fire recruiting websites to attract qualified candidates, improve visibility, and achieve recruitment goals. By implementing SEO best practices, including keyword research, on-page optimization, mobile optimization, and local SEO strategies, organizations can increase website traffic, engage potential recruits, and build a strong online presence in the competitive recruitment landscape. By measuring and monitoring SEO performance, identifying areas for improvement, and adapting strategies based on data-driven insights, police and fire departments can optimize their recruitment efforts and attract the next generation of dedicated first responders.

CHAPTER 9: IMPLEMENTING ADVERTISING ON GOOGLE AND BING TO REACH GENERATION Z IN RECRUITING EFFORTS FOR FIRE & POLICE DEPARTMENTS

In today's digital age, reaching Generation Z (Gen Z), the youngest cohort in the workforce, requires strategic and targeted advertising efforts on platforms where they spend the most time. Google and Bing are two of the most popular search engines used by Gen Z individuals to search for information, including job opportunities.Let's explore how to effectively implement advertising on Google and Bing to reach Generation Z in recruiting efforts for fire and police departments.

Understanding Generation Z: Characteristics and Preferences

Digital Natives: Generation Z is the first generation to grow up entirely in the digital age, surrounded by technology from a young age. They are highly proficient in using smartphones, social media, and search engines to access information and connect with others.

Mobile-First Mindset: Gen Z individuals are mobile-first consumers, preferring to use smartphones and tablets to browse the internet and engage with content. Mobile-friendly advertising campaigns are essential for reaching this audience effectively.

Visual and Interactive Content: Generation Z gravitates towards visual and interactive content that is engaging and shareable. Advertisements that incorporate videos, images, and interactive elements are more likely to capture their attention and resonate with them.

Authenticity and Transparency: Gen Z values authenticity and transparency in advertising. They are quick to identify and reject inauthentic or manipulative content and prefer brands and organizations that communicate openly and honestly.

Advertising on Google: Strategies and Best Practices

Google Ads Platform: Google Ads is a powerful advertising platform that allows organizations to create and manage campaigns across various Google properties, including the Google Search Network, Display Network, and YouTube. This also includes advertising on mobile phone apps as well as video games.

Targeting Options: Google Ads offers a range of targeting options to reach Generation Z individuals effectively. This includes demographic targeting based on age, gender, and location, as well as interests, behaviors, and search intent.

Keywords and Search Intent: Keyword research is essential for identifying the search terms and phrases that Gen Z individuals are using to find information about public safety careers. Target relevant keywords related to fire and police recruitment to ensure that ads appear in relevant search results.

Compelling Ad Copy: Craft compelling ad copy that resonates with Generation Z and highlights the benefits and opportunities of working in the fire or police department. Use clear and concise language, and include a compelling call to action to encourage clicks and engagement. Include story-based messaging in your ad copy to invoke an emotional response.

Mobile Optimization: Optimize ads for mobile devices to ensure a seamless user experience for Generation Z individuals who are browsing on smartphones and tablets. Use responsive design, fast loading times, and mobile-friendly ad formats to maximize engagement and conversions.

Advertising on Bing: Strategies and Best Practices

Bing Ads Platform: Bing Ads is Microsoft's advertising platform, which allows organizations to create and manage campaigns across the Bing search engine and its partner networks, including Yahoo and AOL.

Audience Targeting: Bing Ads offers audience targeting options to reach Generation Z individuals based on demographic, geographic, and behavioral factors. Use audience targeting features to segment and reach specific audience segments effectively.

Keyword Research and Optimization: Conduct keyword research to identify relevant search terms and phrases that Generation Z individuals are using on the Bing search engine. Optimize ad campaigns for targeted keywords to improve visibility and relevance in search results.

Ad Creative and Messaging: Develop ad creative and messaging that resonates with Generation Z and communicates the unique value proposition of working in the fire or police department. Use engaging visuals, compelling copy, and clear calls to action to drive clicks and conversions. Utilize story-based creatives to invoke an emotional response.

Performance Tracking and Optimization: Monitor the performance of Bing Ads campaigns regularly and make adjustments based on key performance indicators (KPIs) such as click-through rates, conversion rates, and return on investment (ROI). Optimize campaigns for better results and allocate budget to top-performing keywords and ad groups.

Integrating Google and Bing Advertising Strategies

Cross-Platform Consistency: Maintain consistency in branding, messaging, and targeting across Google and Bing advertising campaigns to provide a cohesive and seamless experience for Generation Z individuals. Ensure that ads are consistent with other recruitment efforts and reflect the organization's values and culture.

A/B Testing and Experimentation: Conduct A/B testing and experimentation to identify the most effective ad creatives, messaging, and targeting strategies for reaching Generation Z on both Google and Bing. Test different ad formats, copy variations, and targeting options to optimize campaign performance over time.

Conversion Tracking and Attribution: Implement conversion tracking and attribution models to measure the impact of Google and Bing advertising campaigns on recruitment outcomes. Track conversions such as job applications, website visits, and sign-ups to evaluate campaign effectiveness and allocate budget accordingly.

Continuous Optimization and Improvement: Continuously optimize and refine Google and Bing advertising campaigns based on performance data and insights. Monitor trends, identify opportunities for improvement, and adapt strategies to stay ahead of changes in search behavior and audience preferences.

Advertising on Google and Bing offers powerful opportunities to reach Generation Z individuals and attract them to careers in the fire and police departments. By understanding the characteristics and preferences of Gen Z, implementing targeted advertising strategies on both platforms, and continuously optimizing campaigns for better results, organizations can effectively engage potential recruits and build a pipeline of talented first responders. With a strategic approach to advertising on Google and Bing, fire and police departments can reach Generation Z where they are most active online, and inspire them to join the ranks of public safety professionals.

Optimizing Ad Content and Visuals for Maximum Visibility to Reach Generation Z in Fire & Police Recruiting

In the competitive landscape of recruitment, reaching Generation Z (Gen Z) individuals requires strategic and visually appealing advertising content. As digital natives, Gen Z individuals are highly accustomed to engaging with visual content on various online platforms. To effectively attract their attention and interest in fire and police recruiting efforts, it's crucial to optimize ad content and visuals for maximum visibility. Let's explore strategies for optimizing ad content and visuals to reach Generation Z in fire and police recruiting campaigns.

Understanding Generation Z: Preferences and Behaviors

Visual-Centric Consumption: Generation Z individuals are known for their preference for visual content. They are more likely to engage with images, videos, and graphics compared to text-heavy content. Leveraging visually appealing ad content is essential to capturing their attention and maintaining engagement.

Short Attention Spans: Gen Z individuals have shorter attention spans, often due to their exposure to a constant stream of information on social media and other digital platforms. Ad content needs to be concise, compelling, and visually stimulating to quickly grab their attention and convey the message effectively.

Authenticity and Transparency: Gen Z values authenticity and transparency in advertising. They are quick to recognize and reject overly polished or inauthentic content. Advertisements that feel genuine, relatable, and honest are more likely to resonate with this audience.

Mobile-First Mindset: Generation Z is predominantly mobile-first, with smartphones being their primary device for accessing the internet. Ad content should be optimized for mobile devices, with responsive design, fast loading times, and mobile-friendly formats to ensure maximum visibility and engagement.

Crafting Compelling Ad Copy

Concise and Clear Messaging: Keep ad copy concise and clear, conveying the message succinctly and directly. Use short sentences and bullet points to highlight key points and benefits of working in the fire or police department.

Highlighting Benefits and Opportunities: Focus on the unique benefits and opportunities offered by a career in public safety. Highlight aspects such as job stability, career advancement, training programs, and the opportunity to make a positive impact on the community. Remember to keep the recruit as the hero and the department as the guide to achieving personal success.

Incorporating Keywords: Incorporate relevant keywords and phrases into ad copy to improve visibility in search results. Use terms that resonate with Gen Z individuals and align with their search intent when looking for job opportunities in the fire and police departments.

Including a Clear Call to Action: Every ad should include a clear call to action that prompts Gen Z individuals to take the desired action, whether it's applying for a job, attending a recruitment event, or contacting the recruitment team for more information. Use actionable language and compelling incentives to encourage engagement.

Designing Engaging Visuals

High-Quality Images and Videos: Use high-quality images and videos that are visually appealing and relevant to the fire and police recruitment theme. Showcasing real-life scenarios, training exercises, and community engagement activities can help convey the excitement and importance of a career in public safety.

Authentic and Relatable Imagery: Choose images and videos that feel authentic and relatable to Gen Z individuals. Avoid using stock photos or staged imagery that may come across as inauthentic. Instead, opt for real-life visuals that depict diverse and inclusive representations of firefighters and police officers.

Storytelling Through Visuals: Use visuals to tell a story and evoke emotion in Gen Z individuals. Showcasing real stories of firefighters and police officers in action, along with testimonials from current recruits, can help create a connection and inspire interest in a career in public safety.

Interactive and Dynamic Elements: Incorporate interactive and dynamic elements into ad visuals to increase engagement and captivate Gen Z individuals' attention. This could include interactive graphics, animations, or immersive experiences that allow users to explore different aspects of the recruitment process.

Optimizing for Social Media Platforms

Platform-Specific Optimization: Tailor ad content and visuals for different social media platforms based on their unique features and audience demographics. Customize ad formats, dimensions, and messaging to align with the preferences and behaviors of Gen Z users on each platform.

Leveraging Stories and Reels: Utilize features such as Instagram Stories and TikTok Reels to create short-form, visually engaging content that captures Gen Z individuals' attention. These formats offer immersive, full-screen experiences that are ideal for showcasing behind-the-scenes content and day-in-the-life stories of firefighters and police officers.

User-Generated Content: Encourage user-generated content from current recruits, employees, and community members to add authenticity and credibility to fire and police recruiting efforts. Share user-generated photos, videos, and testimonials on social media platforms to showcase real experiences and perspectives.

Engaging with the Audience: Foster engagement with Gen Z individuals by responding to comments, messages, and inquiries promptly. Encourage dialogue, ask questions, and invite feedback to create a sense of community and involvement in fire and police recruitment campaigns.

Incorporating Diversity and Inclusion

Representation Matters: Ensure that ad content and visuals reflect the diversity and inclusivity of the fire and police departments. Showcasing diverse representations of firefighters and police officers can help attract Gen Z individuals from all backgrounds and demographics. Try to be genuine in your intent and avoid the "hey look at our minorities" creatives.

Celebrating Diversity: Celebrate diversity and inclusion in ad campaigns by highlighting the unique perspectives, experiences, and contributions of individuals from different ethnicities, genders, and backgrounds. Use ad visuals to showcase the department's commitment to creating an inclusive and welcoming environment for all recruits.

Empowering Underrepresented Groups: Empower underrepresented groups within the fire and police departments by featuring their stories and achievements in ad content and visuals. Highlighting the experiences of women, minorities, and other marginalized groups can help inspire interest and confidence in a career in public safety.

Optimizing ad content and visuals for maximum visibility is essential for reaching Generation Z in fire and police recruiting efforts. By crafting compelling ad copy, designing engaging visuals, and leveraging social media platforms effectively, organizations can capture the attention and interest of Gen Z individuals and inspire them to consider a career in public safety. Incorporating diversity and inclusion in ad campaigns ensures that fire and police departments appeal to a diverse range of recruits and reflect the values of equality and representation. With a strategic approach to ad optimization, fire and police departments can effectively attract the next generation of dedicated first responders and build a diverse and inclusive workforce.

CHAPTER 10: HARNESSING SOCIAL MEDIA ADS

Overview of Social Media Platforms Best Used to Recruit Generation Z for Fire & Police Departments

Social media has become an indispensable tool for recruitment efforts, especially when targeting Generation Z (Gen Z), the youngest cohort in the workforce. Gen Z individuals are digital natives who spend a significant amount of time on social media platforms, making these platforms essential for reaching and engaging with potential recruits for fire and police departments. In this chapter, we will provide an overview of the social media platforms best used to recruit Generation Z for fire and police departments, highlighting their key features, demographics, and strategies for effective recruitment. Remember that only ads or post-paid boosting will enable you to reach an effective audience. Free unpaid posts are throttled by all social media companies.

Understanding Generation Z's Social Media Habits

The pervasiveness of Social Media: Generation Z individuals are avid users of social media platforms, with the majority spending several hours a day scrolling through their feeds, interacting with content, and connecting with friends and peers.

Diversity of Platform Preferences: While certain social media platforms are more popular among Gen Z individuals, their preferences can vary based on factors such as age, interests, and cultural background. It's essential to understand these preferences to tailor recruitment efforts effectively.

Preference for Visual Content: Gen Z individuals gravitate towards visual content, including images, videos, and infographics. Platforms that offer visually engaging features such as stories, reels, and live streaming are particularly effective for capturing their attention.

Importance of Authenticity and Transparency: Gen Z values authenticity and transparency in social media content. They are more likely to engage with brands and organizations that share genuine, relatable, and authentic content rather than overly polished or promotional material.

Overview of Social Media Platforms for Recruitment

Instagram

Key Features: Instagram is a visual-centric platform that allows users to share photos, videos, and stories. It also offers features such as reels for short-form video content and IGTV for longer videos.

<u>Demographics:</u> Instagram is popular among Gen Z individuals, with a significant portion of its user base falling within the 18-24 age range. It also has a high concentration of users in urban areas.

<u>Recruitment Strategies:</u> Use Instagram to showcase behind-the-scenes glimpses of life in the fire and police departments, highlight employee stories and testimonials, and share engaging visual content that resonates with Gen Z individuals.

TikTok

<u>Key Features:</u> TikTok is a short-form video platform known for its viral challenges, trends, and creative content. Users can create and share videos up to 60 seconds long, often set to music or audio clips.

<u>Demographics:</u> TikTok has a predominantly young user base, with Gen Z individuals comprising a significant portion of its audience. It is particularly popular among teens and young adults who enjoy consuming and creating entertaining content.

<u>Recruitment Strategies:</u> Leverage TikTok's creative features to showcase the excitement and challenges of working in the fire and police departments. Create engaging and entertaining videos that highlight the unique aspects of public safety careers and encourage user participation through challenges and duets. Many Gen Z'ers report that TikTok is their source for local and international news.

Snapchat

<u>Key Features:</u> Snapchat is a multimedia messaging app known for its disappearing messages, filters, and lenses. It offers features such as stories for sharing ephemeral content and Discover for curated content from publishers and creators.

<u>Demographics:</u> Snapchat has a large Gen Z user base, with the majority of its users being under the age of 25. It is particularly

popular among younger teens and college students.

Recruitment Strategies: Use Snapchat to share behind-the-scenes content, host Q&A sessions with current recruits or employees, and create interactive experiences such as augmented reality (AR) lenses that allow users to try on uniforms or participate in virtual training exercises.

YouTube

Key Features: YouTube is a video-sharing platform that allows users to upload, view, and share videos on a wide range of topics. It offers features such as live streaming, premieres, and a community tab for engaging with subscribers.

Demographics: YouTube has a diverse user base, with a significant portion of its audience being Gen Z individuals. It is popular among teens and young adults who use the platform to consume educational, entertainment, and lifestyle content. YouTube is also the second largest search engine behind Google. YouTube is owned by Google. Many potential recruits are searching YouTube for career opportunities and to learn more about options.

Recruitment Strategies: Create informative and engaging video content that provides insights into the recruitment process, highlights career opportunities, and showcases the experiences of firefighters and police officers. Utilize YouTube's advertising options to reach a broader audience and promote recruitment videos.

Twitter

Key Features: Twitter is a microblogging platform that allows users to share short, text-based posts known as tweets. It also offers features such as images, videos, and polls for engaging with followers.

Demographics: Twitter has a diverse user base, including a

significant portion of Gen Z individuals. It is popular among users who are interested in news, current events, and trending topics.

Recruitment Strategies: Use Twitter to share real-time updates, news, and announcements related to fire and police recruitment efforts. Engage with followers through interactive content such as polls and Q&A sessions, and participate in relevant conversations using trending hashtags.

Developing a Social Media Recruitment Strategy

Define Objectives and Goals: Determine specific recruitment objectives and goals for each social media platform, such as increasing awareness, driving website traffic, or generating applications. Align these goals with the overall recruitment strategy for fire and police departments.

Identify Target Audience: Identify the target audience of Gen Z individuals on each social media platform based on demographics, interests, and behaviors. Tailor content and messaging to resonate with the preferences and characteristics of each audience segment.

Create Compelling Content: Develop engaging and visually appealing content that captures the attention of Gen Z individuals and communicates the value proposition of working in the fire and police departments. Experiment with different formats, including images, videos, stories, and interactive elements.

Leverage Influencer Partnerships: Collaborate with influencers, creators, and ambassadors who have a strong presence and following on social media platforms popular among Gen Z individuals. Partnering with influencers can help amplify reach, credibility, and engagement with recruitment content.

Engage and Interact: Foster engagement and interaction with Gen Z individuals by responding to comments, messages, and inquiries promptly. Encourage user-generated content, feedback, and participation to create a sense of community and involvement in fire and police recruitment efforts.

Monitoring and Evaluation

Track Key Metrics: Monitor key metrics and performance indicators to evaluate the effectiveness of social media recruitment efforts. This may include metrics such as reach, engagement, click-through rates, conversion rates, and applicant demographics.

Analyze Insights and Data: Analyze insights and data from social media platforms to gain insights into audience behavior, preferences, and trends. Use this information to refine content strategy, optimize ad targeting, and make data-driven decisions for future recruitment campaigns.

Measure Return on Investment: Calculate the return on investment (ROI) of social media recruitment efforts by comparing the cost of advertising and content creation to the outcomes achieved, such as the number of applications received or recruits hired. Adjust budget allocation and strategies based on ROI analysis.

Continuous Improvement: Continuously monitor, evaluate, and refine social media recruitment strategies to optimize performance and achieve recruitment goals. Stay informed about changes in platform algorithms, user behavior, and industry trends to adapt strategies accordingly.

Social media platforms offer powerful opportunities to recruit Generation Z individuals for fire and police departments by providing a direct and engaging way to reach and interact with potential recruits. By understanding the unique features, demographics, and preferences of each platform, organizations can develop tailored recruitment strategies that effectively engage and inspire Gen Z individuals to consider a career in public safety. With a strategic approach to social media recruitment, fire and police departments can attract a diverse and talented pool of recruits who are passionate about serving and protecting their communities.

Targeting Gen Z and Millennials Through Social Media Ads

In the ever-evolving landscape of digital marketing, social media platforms have emerged as powerful tools for reaching and engaging with Generation Z (Gen Z) and millennials. These two demographic groups, born between the mid-1990s and the early 2010s, are digital natives who spend a significant amount of time on social media platforms. To effectively target Gen Z and millennials through social media ads, it's essential to understand their preferences, behaviors, and habits on various platforms. Let's explore strategies for targeting Gen Z and millennials through social media ads, focusing on key platforms, audience segmentation, ad formats, and optimization techniques.

Understanding Gen Z and Millennials on Social Media

Digital Natives: Gen Z and millennials are digital natives who have grown up in a world dominated by technology and social media. They are highly proficient in using smartphones, tablets, and social media platforms to communicate, consume content, and engage with brands.

Mobile-First Consumers: Both Gen Z and millennials are predominantly mobile-first consumers, with smartphones being their primary devices for accessing the internet and social media. They prefer mobile-friendly content and experiences that are optimized for smaller screens and on-the-go consumption.

Preference for Visual Content: Gen Z and millennials gravitate towards visual content, including images, videos, and infographics, that is engaging, entertaining, and shareable. They are more likely to engage with ads that feature compelling visuals and storytelling elements.

Desire for Authenticity and Personalization: Gen Z and millennials value authenticity and personalization in social media ads. They prefer ads that feel genuine, relatable, and tailored to their interests and preferences, rather than generic or impersonal content.

Targeting Strategies for Gen Z and Millennials

Audience Segmentation: Segment the target audience of Gen Z and millennials based on demographics, interests, behaviors, and psychographics. Use data from social media platforms, such as age, gender, location, interests, and engagement patterns, to create detailed audience segments.

Custom Audiences: Create custom audiences of Gen Z and

millennials based on existing recruit data, such as email lists, website visitors, and app users. Use retargeting ads to re-engage with users who have previously interacted with your brand or shown interest in your department or positions.

Lookalike Audiences: Expand the reach of social media ads by creating lookalike audiences of Gen Z and millennials who share similar characteristics and behaviors to your existing recruit base. Use lookalike audience targeting to reach new prospects who are likely to be interested in your department.

Interest and Behavior Targeting: Target Gen Z and millennials based on their interests, hobbies, and behaviors on social media platforms. Use targeting options such as interests, hobbies, pages liked, groups joined, and events attended to reach users who are most likely to be interested in your ads.

Ad Formats and Creative Strategies

Visual Ads: Use visually appealing images and videos in social media ads to capture the attention of Gen Z and millennials. Showcase the department, the services, or experiences in a visually compelling way that resonates with the interests and preferences of the target audience.

Video Ads: Create short-form video ads that are engaging, entertaining, and informative. Use storytelling, humor, and creativity to captivate Gen Z and millennials and convey your brand message effectively within a limited timeframe.

Carousel Ads: Utilize carousel ads to showcase multiple images in a single ad unit. This allows you to provide more information and options to Gen Z and millennials, increasing engagement and driving conversions.

Interactive Ads: Experiment with interactive ad formats such as polls, quizzes, and augmented reality (AR) experiences to engage Gen Z and millennials in a more interactive and immersive way. Encourage participation and feedback to create a sense of involvement and ownership.

Optimization and Performance Tracking

A/B Testing: Conduct A/B testing to compare different ad creatives, messaging, and targeting strategies and identify the most effective combinations for reaching Gen Z and millennials. Test variables such as ad copy, visuals, calls to action, and audience segments to optimize campaign performance.

Performance Tracking: Monitor key performance indicators (KPIs) such as reach, engagement, click-through rates, conversion rates, and return on ad spend (ROAS) to evaluate the effectiveness of social media ads targeting Gen Z and millennials. Use analytics and reporting tools provided by social media platforms to track and analyze ad performance.

Audience Insights: Gain insights into the preferences, behaviors, and trends of Gen Z and millennials through audience analytics provided by social media platforms. Use these insights to refine targeting, optimize ad content, and tailor messaging to better resonate with the target audience.

Continuous Optimization: Continuously optimize social media ad campaigns targeting Gen Z and millennials based on performance data and insights. Adjust targeting parameters, ad creatives, and bidding strategies to maximize ROI and achieve campaign objectives effectively.

Targeting Gen Z and millennials through social media ads requires a deep understanding of their preferences, behaviors, and habits on various platforms. By leveraging audience segmentation, choosing the right social media platforms, and implementing creative ad formats and optimization techniques, marketers can effectively reach and engage with these demographic groups. With a strategic approach to social media advertising, businesses can drive brand awareness, engagement, and conversions among Gen Z and millennials, ultimately contributing to the success and growth of their marketing efforts.

Creating Engaging Ad Content and Visual Media to Capture the Attention of Gen Z and Millennials

In the fast-paced world of digital advertising, capturing the attention of Generation Z (Gen Z) and millennials requires more than just traditional marketing techniques. These tech-savvy and digitally native demographic groups demand engaging and visually appealing content that resonates with their interests, values, and preferences. Let's explore strategies for creating compelling ad content and visual media to capture the attention of Gen Z and millennials, focusing on key principles, formats, and tactics for success.

Understanding the Preferences of Gen Z and Millennials

Visual-Centric Consumption: Gen Z and millennials prefer visual content over text-heavy material. They are drawn to images, videos, and infographics that are visually appealing, immersive, and shareable.

Authenticity and Transparency: Both Gen Z and millennials value authenticity and transparency in advertising. They are skeptical of overly polished or inauthentic content and prefer ads that feel genuine, relatable, and honest.

Personalization and Relevance: Gen Z and millennials expect personalized and relevant content that speaks to their unique interests, needs, and aspirations. They are more likely to engage with ads that are tailored to their preferences and lifestyles.

Mobile-First Mindset: Gen Z and millennials are predominantly mobile-first consumers, with smartphones being their primary devices for accessing the internet and social media. Ad content should be optimized for mobile devices and deliver a seamless user experience.

Principles of Creating Engaging Ad Content

Storytelling: Use storytelling techniques to create narratives that captivate and resonate with Gen Z and millennials. Develop characters, plotlines, and conflicts that evoke emotion and intrigue, keeping viewers engaged from beginning to end.

Authenticity: Prioritize authenticity and honesty in ad content, showcasing real people, experiences, and stories that reflect the values and culture of your brand. Avoid overly staged or scripted content that may come across as inauthentic or insincere.

Humor and Entertainment: Incorporate humor and entertainment into ad content to grab the attention of Gen Z and millennials and make them more memorable. Use witty jokes, clever puns, and playful humor to create a positive and enjoyable viewing experience.

Interactivity and Engagement: Create interactive ad experiences that encourage participation and engagement from Gen Z and millennials. Incorporate interactive elements such as polls, quizzes, and games that invite viewers to interact with the content and share their opinions.

Visual Media Formats for Engaging Ad Content

Short-Form Videos: Create short-form videos that are concise, entertaining, and attention-grabbing. Keep short-form videos under 60 seconds in length and focus on delivering a clear and compelling message within a limited timeframe.

Long-Form Videos: Create long-form videos that act as documentaries or docuseries about your department, the recruit school process, hero stories, and more. Post this long-form media to YouTube and then post links to it from your social media channels.

Behind-the-Scenes Footage: Offer behind-the-scenes glimpses of your brand, department, or services to provide authenticity and transparency. Showcasing real people and processes can humanize your brand and build trust with Gen Z and millennials.

User-Generated Content: Incorporate user-generated content into ad campaigns to showcase real experiences and testimonials from satisfied recruits or fans. Encourage users to create and share their own content using branded hashtags or challenges.

Visual Graphics

Infographics: Create visually appealing infographics that convey complex information or statistics in a simple and digestible format. Use eye-catching colors, icons, and illustrations to make data more engaging and easy to understand.

Memes and GIFs: Utilize memes and GIFs to inject humor and relatability into ad content and resonate with Gen Z and millennials' internet culture. Choose relevant and trending memes that align with your brand voice and messaging.

Interactive Graphics: Develop interactive graphics and animations that encourage users to explore and interact with content. Use interactive elements such as sliders, scroll effects, and clickable hotspots to enhance engagement and immersion.

Social Media Stories

Instagram Stories: Utilize Instagram Stories to share ephemeral content that disappears after 24 hours. Create short-lived but engaging stories that provide behind-the-scenes glimpses, job demos, or ride alongs to capture the attention of Gen Z and millennials.

Snapchat Stories: Leverage Snapchat Stories to connect with Gen Z and millennials in a more casual and authentic way. Use creative filters, stickers, and geolocation tags to enhance storytelling and engage with followers in real time.

Tactics for Creating Engaging Ad Content

Use Eye-Catching Visuals: Incorporate high-quality images, videos, and graphics that grab the attention of Gen Z and millennials as they scroll through their social media feeds. Use bold colors, striking imagery, and compelling compositions to stand out from the competition.

Optimize for Mobile Devices: Ensure that ad content is optimized for mobile devices, with responsive design, fast loading times, and mobile-friendly formats. Keep text concise and legible, and use large, clickable buttons and calls to action for easy navigation on small screens.

Leverage User-Generated Content: Encourage user-generated content from recruits, fans, and followers to add authenticity and social proof to ad campaigns. Feature user-generated photos, videos, and testimonials in ads to showcase real experiences and build trust with Gen Z and millennials.

Test and Iterate: Continuously test and iterate ad content to optimize performance and maximize engagement with Gen Z and millennials. Experiment with different formats, messaging, and targeting strategies to identify what resonates best with your target audience.

Creating engaging ad content and visual media is essential for capturing the attention of Generation Z and millennials in today's competitive digital landscape. By understanding their preferences, values, and behaviors, marketers can develop ad campaigns that resonate with these demographic groups and drive meaningful engagement and interactions. By leveraging storytelling, authenticity, humor, and interactivity, brands can create memorable and impactful ad experiences that leave a lasting impression on Gen Z and millennials. With a strategic approach to ad content creation and optimization, recruiters can effectively connect with these tech-savvy and visually oriented audiences and achieve their marketing objectives in the digital age.

CHAPTER 11: EXPLORING PROGRAMMATIC ADVERTISING

In the ever-evolving landscape of digital advertising, programmatic advertising has emerged as a powerful and efficient way for marketers to reach their target audience at scale. Programmatic advertising leverages technology and data to automate the buying and selling of digital ad inventory in real time, allowing advertisers to deliver highly targeted and personalized ads to their desired audience. In this chapter, we will explore the fundamentals of programmatic advertising, its key components, and the benefits it offers to advertisers.

What is Programmatic Advertising?

Definition: Programmatic advertising refers to the automated buying and selling of digital ad inventory through real-time bidding (RTB) platforms and algorithms. It allows advertisers to reach their target audience across a wide range of digital channels, including display, video, social media, and mobile, using data-driven targeting and optimization techniques.

Key Components:

Demand-Side Platform (DSP): A DSP is a technology platform that enables advertisers to purchase ad inventory across multiple publishers and ad exchanges through real-time bidding. Advertisers can set targeting criteria, bid on ad impressions, and optimize campaign performance within a DSP.

Supply-Side Platform (SSP): An SSP is a technology platform used by publishers to manage and sell their ad inventory to advertisers. SSPs connect publishers with ad exchanges and DSPs, allowing them to maximize revenue by selling ad impressions at the highest possible price.

Ad Exchange: An ad exchange is a digital marketplace where publishers and advertisers come together to buy and sell ad inventory in real-time. Ad exchanges facilitate the auction-based buying and selling of ad impressions through RTB platforms, ensuring efficient and transparent transactions.

Data Management Platform (DMP): A DMP is a technology platform that aggregates, analyzes, and activates audience data for targeting and personalization purposes. DMPs collect and organize data from various sources, including cookies, mobile IDs, and third-party data providers, to create audience segments for targeting in programmatic advertising campaigns.

Benefits of Programmatic Advertising

Targeted Advertising: Programmatic advertising allows advertisers to target their ads with precision, reaching specific audiences based on demographics, interests, behaviors, and intent signals. Advertisers can leverage first-party, second-party, and third-party data to create highly customized audience segments and deliver relevant ads to their target audience.

Real-Time Optimization: Programmatic advertising enables real-time optimization of ad campaigns, allowing advertisers to adjust targeting, bidding, and creative elements on the fly to maximize performance. Advertisers can monitor campaign metrics in real time and make data-driven decisions to improve ROI and achieve their advertising objectives.

Increased Efficiency: Programmatic advertising streamlines the ad buying process, eliminating manual tasks and inefficiencies associated with traditional advertising methods. Advertisers can access a vast inventory of ad placements and audiences through a single platform, saving time and resources compared to manual ad buying.

Enhanced Reach and Scale: Programmatic advertising provides access to a vast ecosystem of digital publishers, ad exchanges, and ad networks, allowing advertisers to reach their target audience across a wide range of channels and devices. Advertisers can scale their campaigns and extend their reach to new audiences with ease, driving brand awareness and engagement at scale.

Improved Transparency and Control: Programmatic advertising offers greater transparency and control over ad placements, pricing, and performance metrics. Advertisers have visibility into where their ads are being displayed, how much they are paying for ad impressions, and the performance of their campaigns, allowing them to optimize their ad spend and achieve better results.

Advanced Targeting Capabilities: Programmatic advertising enables advanced targeting capabilities, including contextual targeting, geographic targeting, device targeting, and retargeting. Advertisers can tailor their ad campaigns to specific audiences and contexts, delivering personalized messaging and offers that resonate with their target audience.

Cost-Effectiveness: Programmatic advertising offers cost-effective pricing models, including cost-per-thousand-impressions (CPM), cost-per-click (CPC), and cost-per-action (CPA). Advertisers can optimize their bidding strategies and ad placements to achieve their desired outcomes while minimizing costs and maximizing ROI.

Data-Driven Insights: Programmatic advertising provides access to rich data and insights that can inform marketing strategies and decision-making. Advertisers can analyze campaign performance metrics, audience behavior, and market trends to gain valuable insights into their target audience and optimize future campaigns for success.

Best Practices for Programmatic Advertising

Define Clear Objectives: Clearly define your advertising objectives, target audience, and key performance indicators (KPIs) before launching a programmatic advertising campaign. Align your objectives with your overall marketing strategy and business goals to ensure success.

Segment Your Audience: Segment your target audience into distinct segments based on demographics, interests, behaviors, and purchase intent. Create customized audience segments for different stages of the recruiting journey and tailor your ad messaging and creative accordingly.

Test and Iterate: Test different ad formats, messaging, targeting criteria, and bidding strategies to identify what resonates best with your target audience. Continuously monitor campaign performance metrics and make data-driven optimizations to improve ROI and achieve your advertising objectives.

Monitor Brand Safety: Ensure brand safety by monitoring ad placements and avoiding placement on websites or content that may be deemed inappropriate or harmful to your brand image. Use brand safety tools and technologies to mitigate the risk of ad fraud, invalid traffic, and brand reputation issues.

Leverage Data and Insights: Leverage data and insights from your programmatic advertising campaigns to inform marketing strategies and decision-making. Analyze campaign performance metrics, audience behavior, and market trends to identify opportunities for optimization and growth.

Programmatic advertising offers advertisers a powerful and efficient way to reach their target audience with precision and scale across digital channels. By leveraging technology, data, and automation, advertisers can deliver highly targeted and personalized ads to their desired audience, driving brand awareness, engagement, and conversions. With its numerous benefits, including targeted advertising, real-time optimization, increased efficiency, and enhanced reach and scale, programmatic advertising is becoming an indispensable tool for marketers looking to achieve their advertising objectives in the digital age. By understanding the fundamentals of programmatic advertising and implementing best practices, advertisers can unlock the full potential of this transformative advertising technology and drive meaningful results for their businesses.

Utilizing Programmatic Advertising to Reach Gen Z and Millennials

In the rapidly evolving landscape of digital marketing, reaching Generation Z (Gen Z) and millennials poses unique challenges for advertisers. These tech-savvy and digitally native demographic groups have grown up in an era dominated by technology and social media, making traditional advertising methods less effective in capturing their attention. To effectively engage Gen Z and millennials, advertisers must leverage innovative and targeted approaches, such as programmatic advertising. Let's explore how programmatic advertising can be utilized to reach Gen Z and millennials, focusing on strategies, best practices, and case studies.

Leveraging Programmatic Advertising to Reach Gen Z and Millennials

Targeted Advertising: Programmatic advertising allows advertisers to target their ads with precision, reaching specific audiences based on demographics, interests, behaviors, and intent signals. Advertisers can leverage first-party, second-party, and third-party data to create highly customized audience segments and deliver relevant ads to Gen Z and millennials.

Contextual Targeting: Programmatic advertising enables contextual targeting, allowing advertisers to deliver ads based on the content and context of the webpage or app. Advertisers can target Gen Z and millennials with ads that are relevant to the content they are consuming, increasing the likelihood of engagement and conversion.

Dynamic Creative Optimization (DCO): Programmatic advertising supports dynamic creative optimization (DCO), allowing advertisers to personalize ad creative in real time based on user data and behavior. Advertisers can deliver personalized ad experiences to Gen Z and millennials, increasing relevance and effectiveness.

Cross-Device Targeting: Programmatic advertising enables cross-device targeting, allowing advertisers to reach Gen Z and millennials across multiple devices, including smartphones, tablets, desktops, and connected TVs. Advertisers can deliver seamless and consistent ad experiences across all digital touchpoints, maximizing reach and engagement.

Real-Time Optimization: Programmatic advertising enables real-time optimization of ad campaigns, allowing advertisers to adjust targeting, bidding, and creative elements on the fly to maximize performance. Advertisers can monitor campaign metrics in real time and make data-driven decisions to improve ROI and achieve their advertising objectives.

Programmatic advertising offers advertisers a powerful and efficient way to reach Gen Z and millennials with precision and scale across digital channels. By leveraging technology, data, and automation, advertisers can deliver highly targeted and personalized ads to their desired audience, driving brand awareness, engagement, and conversions. With its numerous benefits, including targeted advertising, contextual targeting, real-time optimization, and cross-device targeting, programmatic advertising is becoming an indispensable tool for marketers looking to engage Gen Z and millennials in today's digital landscape. By understanding the preferences, behaviors, and habits of Gen Z and millennials, and implementing best practices for programmatic advertising, advertisers can unlock the full potential of this transformative advertising technology and achieve their marketing objectives in the digital age.

Optimizing Ad Placements and Budgets for Effective Police & Fire Recruiting

In today's competitive job market, recruiting qualified candidates for police and fire departments requires strategic and targeted advertising efforts. With the rise of digital marketing channels, recruiters have access to a variety of platforms and tools to reach potential recruits effectively. Let's explore the importance of optimizing ad placements and budgets for police and fire recruiting campaigns, focusing on strategies, best practices, and case studies.

Understanding the Recruitment Landscape for Police & Fire Departments

Recruitment Challenges: Police and fire departments face unique challenges in recruiting qualified candidates, including competition from other employers, public perception issues, and stringent hiring requirements. These challenges necessitate a proactive and targeted approach to recruitment marketing.

Importance of Digital Marketing: Digital marketing has become increasingly important in police and fire recruiting efforts, offering a cost-effective way to reach potential recruits and engage with them on platforms they frequent.

Target Audience: The target audience for police and fire recruiting campaigns includes individuals who are interested in public service, have the necessary qualifications, and align with the values and mission of the respective departments. Understanding the demographics, interests, and behaviors of this audience is crucial for effective targeting.

Optimizing Ad Placements for Police & Fire Recruiting

Targeted Platforms: Identify the most relevant digital platforms for reaching potential recruits, such as job boards, social media platforms, and niche websites catering to public safety professionals. Tailor your ad placements to the preferences and habits of your target audience.

Social Media Advertising: Leverage social media platforms like Facebook, Instagram, and LinkedIn to target specific demographics, interests, and behaviors relevant to police and fire recruiting. Use targeted ads, sponsored content, and promoted posts to reach potential recruits and drive engagement.

Job Boards and Niche Websites: Partner with job boards and niche websites that specialize in public safety recruitment to reach a highly targeted audience of qualified candidates. Advertise job openings and recruitment events on these platforms to attract individuals with relevant skills and experience.

Search Engine Marketing (SEM): Utilize search engine marketing tactics, such as Google Ads and Bing Ads, to target individuals actively searching for police and fire department jobs. Bid on relevant keywords and phrases related to public safety careers to ensure visibility in search engine results.

Programmatic Advertising: Consider utilizing programmatic advertising platforms to automate the buying and placement of digital ads across a variety of channels and websites. Programmatic advertising can help optimize ad placements based on audience data and performance metrics, ensuring maximum reach and efficiency.

Best Practices for Optimizing Ad Placements

<u>Audience Targeting:</u> Define your target audience based on demographics, interests, and behaviors relevant to police and fire recruiting. Use audience targeting features available on digital advertising platforms to reach individuals who are most likely to be interested in public safety careers.

<u>Geographic Targeting:</u> Tailor your ad placements to specific geographic locations where you are actively recruiting candidates. Use geotargeting features to focus your advertising efforts on areas with a high concentration of potential recruits or areas where recruitment efforts are currently underway.

<u>Ad Creative and Messaging:</u> Develop compelling ad creative and messaging that highlights the benefits of a career in public safety, such as job stability, competitive salaries, opportunities for advancement, and the chance to make a difference in the community. Use visuals, testimonials, and storytelling to capture the attention of potential recruits and convey your department's unique value proposition.

<u>Ad Placement Optimization:</u> Monitor the performance of your ad placements regularly and optimize your campaigns based on key performance indicators (KPIs) such as click-through rates (CTR), conversion rates, and cost-per-acquisition (CPA). Adjust your ad placements, targeting criteria, and bidding strategies to maximize reach and ROI.

<u>Budget Allocation:</u> Allocate your advertising budget strategically across different digital channels and platforms based on their effectiveness in reaching and engaging with potential recruits. Consider factors such as audience size, competition, and cost-per-engagement (CPE) when determining budget allocations for each channel.

Optimizing ad placements and budgets is essential for effective police and fire recruiting campaigns in today's digital landscape. By strategically targeting relevant platforms, leveraging audience targeting features, and optimizing ad creative and messaging, police and fire departments can reach potential recruits with precision and efficiency. With the right strategies and best practices in place, departments can attract qualified candidates, drive engagement, and ultimately, strengthen their workforce.

CHAPTER 12: PRECISION TARGETING WITH IP TARGETING

In the realm of digital recruiting, IP targeting has emerged as a powerful tool for reaching specific audiences with precision and relevance. IP targeting allows recruiters to deliver tailored messages to users based on their internet protocol (IP) addresses, enabling highly targeted and personalized advertising campaigns. In the context of fire and police recruiting, IP targeting can play a significant role in reaching potential candidates who have demonstrated interest in public safety careers. In this chapter, we will explore the concept of IP targeting, its relevance in fire and police recruiting efforts, and best practices for leveraging this technology effectively.

Understanding IP Targeting

Definition: IP targeting refers to the practice of delivering digital advertisements to specific users based on their IP addresses. Every device connected to the internet is assigned a unique IP address, which can be used to identify the device's geographical location and internet service provider (ISP). Advertisers can leverage IP targeting to deliver ads to users in specific geographic areas or within specific organizations or institutions.

How It Works: IP targeting works by matching a user's IP address to a database of IP addresses associated with specific locations or organizations. Advertisers can then use this information to target users within a certain radius of a physical location, such as a police station or fire department headquarters, or within specific organizations, such as colleges or military bases.

Relevance in Digital Advertising: IP targeting allows advertisers to reach highly targeted audiences with relevant messages based on their location, interests, or affiliations. This level of precision targeting can increase the effectiveness of advertising campaigns by ensuring that ads are delivered to users who are most likely to be interested in the job or position being promoted.

Relevance of IP Targeting in Fire & Police Recruiting

Targeting Local Communities: Fire and police departments often prioritize recruiting candidates from their local communities to ensure that recruits are familiar with the area and have a vested interest in serving the community. IP targeting allows departments to target users within specific geographic areas, such as neighborhoods or zip codes, where recruitment efforts are focused.

Reaching Potential Candidates: IP targeting enables fire and police departments to reach potential candidates who have demonstrated interest in public safety careers. By targeting users who have visited relevant websites or engaged with content related to law enforcement or firefighting, departments can identify and connect with individuals who may be interested in pursuing a career in public safety.

Engaging with Specific Audiences: IP targeting can be used to engage with specific audiences, such as students at colleges or universities with criminal justice or fire science programs, military personnel transitioning to civilian life, or individuals attending community events or job fairs. By delivering targeted messages to these audiences, departments can increase awareness of job opportunities and attract qualified candidates.

Promoting Recruitment Events: IP targeting can be used to promote recruitment events, such as job fairs, information sessions, or physical fitness tests, to users within the vicinity of the event location. By targeting users based on their proximity to the event venue, departments can drive attendance and engagement with recruitment activities.

Best Practices for Leveraging IP Targeting in Fire & Police Recruiting

Define Target Audience: Clearly define the target audience for recruitment efforts, including geographic locations, demographics, interests, and affiliations relevant to public safety careers. Use this information to create tailored messaging and targeting criteria for IP targeting campaigns.

Partner with Digital Marketing Experts: Collaborate with digital marketing experts or agencies with experience in IP targeting and recruitment advertising to develop and execute effective campaigns. Leverage their expertise and insights to maximize the impact of IP targeting efforts and achieve recruitment goals.

Tailor Messaging and Creative: Develop compelling ad creative and messaging that resonates with the target audience and highlights the benefits of a career in public safety. Use imagery, testimonials, and storytelling to engage users and convey the unique value proposition of working for the fire or police department.

Monitor and Optimize Campaign Performance: Monitor the performance of IP targeting campaigns regularly and make data-driven optimizations to improve effectiveness and ROI. Track key performance indicators such as ad impressions, click-through rates, website visits, and conversion metrics to evaluate campaign performance and identify areas for improvement.

Ensure Compliance with Privacy Regulations: Ensure compliance with privacy regulations and guidelines when collecting and using IP address data for targeting purposes. Adhere to best practices for data privacy and transparency to maintain trust and credibility with users and mitigate the risk of regulatory penalties.

IP targeting offers fire and police departments a powerful tool for reaching specific audiences with precision and relevance in their recruiting efforts. By leveraging IP address data to target users based on their location, interests, and affiliations, departments can increase awareness of job opportunities, attract qualified candidates, and strengthen their workforce. With the right strategies, messaging, and partnerships in place, fire and police departments can effectively utilize IP targeting to achieve their recruitment goals and ensure the safety and well-being of their communities.

Targeting Specific Locations and Organizations with IP Targeting for Police and Fire Recruiting

In the competitive landscape of public safety recruitment,

targeting specific locations and organizations is crucial for reaching qualified candidates who are likely to be interested in joining police and fire departments. Leveraging IP targeting, a powerful digital marketing tool, allows recruiters to deliver tailored messages to individuals based on their internet protocol (IP) addresses, enabling precise targeting of desired geographic areas and organizations. Let's delve into the significance of targeting specific locations and organizations using IP targeting for police and fire recruiting, exploring strategies, best practices, and case studies.

Understanding IP Targeting for Police and Fire Recruiting

Definition: IP targeting in the context of police and fire recruiting involves delivering digital advertisements to individuals based on their IP addresses, which can provide insight into their geographical location and affiliations with specific organizations. This allows recruiters to target candidates who are located in certain areas or associated with relevant organizations, such as colleges, military bases, or public safety agencies.

How It Works: IP targeting works by mapping IP addresses to physical locations or organizations through databases and algorithms. Recruiters can specify geographic areas or organizations they wish to target, and ads are served to users within those parameters based on their IP addresses. This enables recruiters to reach individuals who are likely to be interested in public safety careers based on their location or affiliation with relevant organizations.

Relevance in Police and Fire Recruiting: Targeting specific locations and organizations with IP targeting is highly relevant in police and fire recruiting for several reasons:

<u>Geographic Focus:</u> Police and fire departments often prioritize recruiting candidates from specific geographic areas to ensure familiarity with the community and commitment to local public safety needs. IP targeting allows recruiters to focus their advertising efforts on these target areas, maximizing the impact of their campaigns.

<u>Affiliation Targeting:</u> Many individuals interested in public safety careers have affiliations with relevant organizations, such as colleges offering criminal justice programs, military bases with transitioning personnel, or public safety agencies with lateral transfer opportunities. IP targeting enables recruiters to reach these candidates by targeting users associated with these organizations. A good practice is to audit all your past recruits to determine what affiliations those recruits came from. Then target those affiliations moving forward.

<u>Personalized Messaging:</u> By targeting specific locations and organizations, recruiters can deliver personalized messaging that resonates with the unique needs and interests of candidates in those areas or affiliations. This increases the relevance and effectiveness of recruitment advertisements, driving engagement and conversion.

Strategies for Targeting Specific Locations and Organizations with IP Targeting

<u>Define Target Areas:</u> Start by identifying the geographic areas or organizations that align with recruitment objectives and target candidate demographics. This may include specific neighborhoods, cities, counties, colleges, military bases, or public safety agencies where recruitment efforts are focused.

Utilize Geofencing: Geofencing is a technique that uses GPS or RFID technology to create virtual boundaries around physical locations, such as police stations, fire departments, colleges, or military bases. Recruiters can use geofencing to target users within these boundaries with relevant recruitment ads based on their proximity to the target locations.

Partner with Third-Party Data Providers: Collaborate with third-party data providers that specialize in IP targeting and audience segmentation to access comprehensive databases of IP addresses and associated locations or organizations. These data providers can help identify and target relevant audiences based on their location, interests, and affiliations.

Tailor Ad Creative and Messaging: Develop ad creative and messaging that speaks directly to the interests and needs of candidates in specific locations or organizations. Highlight local community involvement, career advancement opportunities, specialized training programs, or other incentives that may resonate with target audiences.

Test and Optimize Campaigns: Continuously monitor and optimize IP targeting campaigns to maximize their effectiveness. Test different targeting parameters, ad formats, messaging variations, and creative elements to identify what resonates best with target audiences and drive desired outcomes.

Best Practices for IP Targeting in Police and Fire Recruiting

Maintain Data Privacy and Compliance: Ensure compliance with data privacy regulations and guidelines when collecting and using IP address data for targeting purposes. Adhere to best practices for data security, transparency, and user consent to protect user privacy and mitigate the risk of regulatory penalties.

Measure and Analyze Performance: Use analytics and reporting tools to measure the performance of IP targeting campaigns and track key performance indicators (KPIs) such as ad impressions, click-through rates, website visits, and conversion metrics. Analyze campaign data to identify trends, insights, and areas for optimization.

Leverage Retargeting: Implement retargeting strategies to re-engage users who have interacted with recruitment ads but have not yet taken action. Serve follow-up ads to these users based on their IP addresses, encouraging them to revisit recruitment websites, attend events, or complete application forms.

Coordinate with Recruitment Events: Coordinate IP targeting campaigns with recruitment events, such as job fairs, information sessions, or physical fitness tests, to amplify their impact. Target users within the vicinity of event locations to drive attendance and engagement with recruitment activities.

Partner with Local Organizations: Collaborate with local organizations, community groups, schools, and businesses to extend the reach of IP targeting campaigns and increase their effectiveness. Partnering with trusted organizations can enhance the credibility and visibility of recruitment efforts within target communities.

IP targeting offers police and fire departments a powerful tool for reaching specific locations and organizations with precision and relevance in their recruiting efforts. By leveraging IP address data to target users based on their geographic location or affiliation with relevant organizations, recruiters can effectively reach qualified candidates who are likely to be interested in public safety careers. With the right strategies, messaging, and partnerships in place, police and fire departments can maximize the impact of IP targeting campaigns and attract top talent to strengthen their workforce and serve their communities effectively.

Utilizing Personalized Messaging for IP Targeted Campaigns in Police and Fire Recruiting

In the realm of public safety recruiting, personalized messaging plays a pivotal role in engaging potential candidates and driving them to take action. By leveraging IP targeting, recruiters can deliver tailored messages to individuals based on their geographic location, interests, and affiliations, increasing the relevance and effectiveness of their recruitment campaigns. Let's explore how to utilize personalized messaging for IP-targeted campaigns in police and fire recruiting, including strategies, best practices, and case studies.

Importance of Personalized Messaging in Recruiting

<u>Building Connections:</u> Personalized messaging allows recruiters to establish a connection with potential candidates by addressing their specific needs, interests, and motivations. By tailoring messages to resonate with individual preferences, recruiters can build rapport and trust with candidates, increasing the likelihood of engagement and conversion.

<u>Increasing Relevance:</u> Personalized messaging ensures that recruitment ads are relevant and meaningful to the recipient, capturing their attention and encouraging them to take action.

By highlighting relevant benefits, incentives, and opportunities, recruiters can demonstrate the value of joining the police or fire department and address potential candidates' concerns or objections.

Driving Engagement: Personalized messaging drives engagement by speaking directly to the interests and aspirations of potential candidates. By conveying a compelling value proposition and addressing candidates' unique needs, recruiters can encourage them to learn more about career opportunities, attend recruitment events, or submit applications.

Strategies for Personalized Messaging in IP-Targeted Campaigns

Segmenting Audiences: Start by segmenting your target audience into distinct groups based on criteria such as geographic location, demographics, interests, and affiliations. Tailor messaging and creative elements to each audience segment to ensure relevance and resonance.

Addressing Local Needs: Personalize messaging to address the specific needs and challenges of candidates in different geographic locations. Highlight local community involvement, career advancement opportunities, or specialized training programs that are relevant to candidates in each area.

Highlighting Career Advantages: Emphasize the unique advantages of a career in public safety, such as job stability, competitive salaries, comprehensive benefits, opportunities for advancement, and the chance to make a difference in the community. Tailor messaging to highlight benefits that are most relevant and compelling to potential candidates.

Leveraging Testimonials and Success Stories: Incorporate testimonials and success stories from current officers or firefighters to provide social proof and demonstrate the rewards and fulfillment of a career in public safety. Use real-life examples to illustrate the impact that officers and firefighters have on their communities and inspire potential candidates to join the force.

Call-to-Action (CTA) Optimization: Customize calls-to-action (CTAs) based on the desired action or outcome of each campaign. Encourage potential candidates to visit recruitment websites, attend information sessions, register for recruitment events, or submit applications by providing clear and compelling CTAs tailored to their interests and preferences.

Best Practices for Personalized Messaging in IP-Targeted Campaigns

Data Collection and Analysis: Collect and analyze data on candidate demographics, interests, and behaviors to inform personalized messaging strategies. Use insights from audience research, website analytics, and previous campaign performance to identify trends, preferences, and opportunities for personalization.

Dynamic Creative Optimization (DCO): Implement dynamic creative optimization (DCO) to automatically generate personalized ad creative based on user data and behavior. Utilize DCO technologies to deliver tailored messages, images, and offers to each audience segment, increasing relevance and engagement.

A/B Testing: Conduct A/B testing to experiment with different messaging variations and creative elements to determine what resonates best with target audiences. Test different headlines, images, copywriting styles, and offers to identify high-performing combinations and optimize campaign effectiveness.

Multichannel Integration: Integrate personalized messaging across multiple digital channels and touchpoints to create a cohesive and immersive recruitment experience. Coordinate messaging and creative elements across display ads, social media posts, email campaigns, and website content to reinforce key messages and increase brand visibility.

Performance Monitoring and Optimization: Monitor the performance of IP-targeted campaigns in real-time and make data-driven optimizations to improve effectiveness and ROI. Track key performance indicators (KPIs) such as ad impressions, click-through rates, website visits, and conversion metrics to evaluate campaign performance and identify areas for improvement.

Personalized messaging is a key component of successful IP-targeted campaigns in police and fire recruiting, enabling recruiters to engage potential candidates with relevant and compelling messages. By segmenting audiences, addressing local needs, highlighting career advantages, leveraging testimonials, and optimizing CTAs, recruiters can create personalized experiences that resonate with candidates and drive them to take action. With the right strategies, best practices, and creative approaches, police and fire departments can effectively utilize personalized messaging to attract top talent.

CHAPTER 13: THE IMPORTANCE OF KEYWORD-TARGETED LANDING PAGES IN RECRUITMENT CAMPAIGNS FOR FIRE & POLICE

In the digital age, effective recruitment campaigns for fire and police departments require a strategic approach to online advertising and landing page optimization. Keyword-targeted landing pages play a crucial role in attracting qualified candidates and guiding them through the application process. In this chapter, we will explore the importance of keyword-targeted landing pages in recruitment campaigns for fire and police departments, including their impact on search engine visibility, candidate experience, and conversion rates.

Enhancing Search Engine Visibility

<u>Importance of Keywords:</u> Keywords are the foundation of search engine optimization (SEO) and play a vital role in determining the visibility of landing pages in search engine results pages (SERPs). By targeting relevant keywords related to public safety careers, fire and police departments can improve their chances of ranking higher in search results and attracting organic traffic. Defining the RIGHT keywords is critical as they serve as the foundation for your entire campaign.

<u>Optimizing Landing Page Content:</u> Keyword-targeted landing pages allow fire and police departments to create content that aligns with the search intent of potential candidates. By incorporating targeted keywords into page titles, headings, meta descriptions, and body content, departments can signal to search engines that their landing pages are relevant to users' queries and increase their chances of being displayed prominently in search results.

<u>Increasing Organic Traffic:</u> Keyword-targeted landing pages can help fire and police departments attract organic traffic from individuals actively searching for public safety career opportunities. By optimizing landing pages for relevant keywords, departments can increase their visibility in organic search results and drive qualified traffic to their recruitment websites, resulting in a higher volume of candidate inquiries and applications.

Improving Candidate Experience

<u>Relevance and Alignment:</u> Keyword-targeted landing pages ensure that candidates are directed to content that is relevant to their search queries and interests. By aligning landing page content with the keywords that users are searching for, departments can provide a seamless and intuitive browsing experience that meets candidates' expectations and increases

engagement.

Clear Call-to-Action (CTA): Effective landing pages feature clear and compelling calls-to-action (CTAs) that prompt candidates to take the desired action, such as submitting an application or signing up for a recruitment event. By strategically placing CTAs and using persuasive language, departments can guide candidates through the application process and encourage them to take the next steps towards joining the fire or police force.

User-Friendly Design: Keyword-targeted landing pages should be designed with the user experience in mind, featuring intuitive navigation, mobile responsiveness, and fast load times. By optimizing landing page design and usability, departments can create a positive first impression and make it easy for candidates to find the information they need to make informed decisions about their career prospects.

Maximizing Conversion Rates

Alignment with User Intent: Keyword-targeted landing pages are designed to align with the specific needs and interests of candidates searching for public safety career opportunities. By presenting relevant information and resources that address candidates' questions and concerns, departments can increase the likelihood of conversion and encourage more candidates to take action.

Tailored Messaging: Landing pages allow fire and police departments to deliver tailored messaging that speaks directly to the motivations and aspirations of potential candidates. By highlighting the benefits of working in public safety, showcasing success stories from current officers or firefighters, and addressing common questions and misconceptions, departments can increase engagement and persuade candidates to submit applications or attend recruitment events.

Tracking and Optimization: Keyword-targeted landing pages provide valuable insights into candidate behavior and engagement, allowing departments to track key performance metrics such as conversion rates, bounce rates, and time on page. By analyzing this data and making data-driven optimizations, departments can continuously improve the effectiveness of their landing pages and maximize their conversion rates over time.

Best Practices for Creating Keyword-Targeted Landing Pages

Conduct Keyword Research: Start by conducting keyword research to identify relevant keywords and search queries related to public safety careers. Use keyword research tools and analytics data to uncover high-volume keywords with low competition and incorporate them into landing page content.

Create Compelling Content: Develop engaging and informative content that addresses the needs and interests of potential candidates. Use persuasive language, storytelling, and multimedia elements to capture candidates' attention and encourage them to explore further.

Optimize On-Page Elements: Optimize on-page elements such as page titles, meta descriptions, headings, and body content to include targeted keywords and improve search engine visibility. Use descriptive and keyword-rich language to convey the relevance and value of the landing page to users.

Optimize Off-Page Elements: Optimize off-page elements such

as meta descriptions, image descriptions, and heading tags. Also, ensure your page is handicap user-friendly so that the visual and hearing impaired can easily use and interact with the site.

Design for Conversion: Design landing pages with conversion optimization in mind, featuring prominent call to action, clear navigation, and minimal distractions. Use A/B testing to experiment with different design elements and messaging variations to identify what resonates best with candidates and drives the highest conversion rates.

Monitor and Iterate: Continuously monitor the performance of keyword-targeted landing pages and make data-driven iterations to improve their effectiveness. Track key metrics such as traffic, engagement, and conversion rates, and use insights from analytics data to refine landing page content, design, and messaging over time.

Keyword-targeted landing pages are essential components of successful recruitment campaigns for fire and police departments, providing a targeted and personalized experience for potential candidates. By optimizing landing page content for relevant keywords, enhancing the candidate experience, and maximizing conversion rates, departments can attract qualified candidates, increase engagement, and build a strong and diverse workforce to serve and protect their communities effectively. With the right strategies, best practices, and ongoing optimization efforts, fire and police departments can leverage keyword-targeted landing pages to achieve their recruitment goals and secure top talent for the future.

Elements of High-Converting Landing Pages

In the digital era, landing pages serve as the cornerstone of effective online marketing campaigns. A well-designed landing page can significantly impact conversion rates, turning visitors into leads or recruits. Let's explore the key elements that contribute to the success of high-converting landing pages. By understanding and implementing these elements, marketers can create landing pages that engage visitors, convey persuasive messages, and drive desired actions.

Hero Statement

Definition: The hero statement is a concise statement that communicates the unique benefits and advantages of the job. It tells visitors why they should choose your department over competitors and how it will allow them to obtain their aspirational identity.

Importance: A clear and compelling hero statement is essential for capturing visitors' attention and persuading them to take action. It sets the tone for the entire landing page and communicates the value of the offer upfront, increasing the likelihood of conversion.

Implementation: Place the value proposition prominently on the landing page, ideally above the fold where it is immediately visible to visitors. Use concise and persuasive language to highlight the key benefits and features of the offer, addressing the needs and desires of the target audience.

Engaging Headline and Subheadings

Headline: The headline is the first thing visitors see when they land on the page, making it crucial for grabbing their attention and encouraging them to continue reading. An engaging headline should be clear, concise, and relevant to the offer, piquing visitors' curiosity and encouraging them to learn more.

Subheadings: Subheadings provide additional context and structure to the landing page content, guiding visitors through the key points and benefits of the offer. Use subheadings to break up the text, highlight important information, and maintain visitors' interest as they scroll down the page.

Implementation: Craft a compelling headline that communicates the main benefit or value proposition of the offer in a concise and attention-grabbing manner. Use subheadings to expand on key points, address common objections, and emphasize the unique advantages of the offer.

Compelling Visuals

Images and Graphics: Visual elements such as images, graphics, and videos play a crucial role in capturing visitors' attention and conveying information quickly and effectively. High-quality visuals can enhance the overall appeal of the landing page and reinforce key messages and benefits. This is not the time to use less experienced designers or assign the task to light-duty personnel to "figure it out".

Implementation: Use relevant and eye-catching images or graphics that align with the offer and resonate with the target audience. Incorporate visual elements strategically throughout the landing page to break up text, create visual interest, and reinforce the value proposition.

Persuasive Copywriting

Clarity and Conciseness: Effective copywriting is clear, concise, and easy to understand. Avoid jargon or overly technical language that may confuse or overwhelm visitors. Instead, focus on communicating key messages and benefits straightforwardly and compellingly.

<u>Benefits-Oriented Messaging:</u> Highlight the benefits of the career rather than just listing features. Focus on how the career will improve lives, solve problems, address needs, and avoid failures. Use persuasive language to evoke emotion and create a sense of urgency or desire.

<u>Social Proof:</u> Incorporate social proof elements such as recruit testimonials, reviews, case studies, or endorsements to build trust and credibility. Social proof provides reassurance to visitors that others have had positive experiences with the career, increasing their confidence and likelihood of conversion.

<u>Implementation:</u> Write compelling copy that communicates the unique value proposition of the job and addresses pain points or desires. Use persuasive language to emphasize benefits, create urgency, and encourage action. Incorporate social proof elements strategically to support key messages and build trust with visitors.

Clear Call-to-Action (CTA)

<u>Definition:</u> The call-to-action (CTA) is the prompt that encourages visitors to take the desired action, such as registering for a job fair, filling out an application, or scheduling a follow-up phone call to answer questions. A clear and compelling CTA is essential for guiding potential recruits through the conversion process and prompting them to take action. Define what happens after they take the action so they know what to expect.

<u>Placement and Design:</u> Place the CTA prominently on the landing page where it is easily visible to visitors, ideally above the fold. Use contrasting colors, compelling language, and persuasive design elements to draw attention to the CTA and make it stand out from the rest of the page.

<u>Clarity and Urgency:</u> Make the CTA clear and specific, clearly indicating what action visitors should take and what they will receive in return. Create a sense of urgency or scarcity by using time-sensitive language or limited-time offers to encourage visitors to act quickly.

<u>Implementation:</u> Design a clear and compelling CTA that prompts visitors to take the desired action, such as clicking a button, filling out a form, or making a purchase. Use persuasive language and design elements to create a sense of urgency and encourage immediate action.

Mobile Optimization

<u>Importance:</u> With the rise of mobile devices, it's essential to ensure that landing pages are optimized for mobile users. Mobile optimization improves the user experience, reduces bounce rates, and increases the likelihood of conversion for visitors accessing the page on smartphones or tablets.

<u>Responsive Design:</u> Use responsive design techniques to ensure that landing pages adapt seamlessly to different screen sizes and devices. Test landing pages on various mobile devices to ensure they display correctly and provide a user-friendly experience for mobile users.

<u>Fast Load Times:</u> Mobile users expect fast load times, so optimize

landing pages for speed by minimizing large images, reducing unnecessary scripts or plugins, and leveraging browser caching and compression techniques. Fast-loading pages improve user satisfaction and increase the likelihood of conversion.

High-converting landing pages are essential for driving successful online marketing campaigns and achieving desired business outcomes. By incorporating clear value propositions, engaging headlines, compelling visuals, persuasive copywriting, clear CTAs, and mobile optimization, marketers can create landing pages that effectively engage visitors, communicate key messages, and drive conversions. With careful planning, testing, and optimization, landing pages can become powerful tools for generating leads, acquiring recruits, and achieving marketing objectives.

Best Practices for A/B Testing and Optimization Techniques for Landing Pages

A/B testing is a powerful technique used by marketers to optimize landing pages and improve conversion rates. By comparing two or more versions of a landing page and analyzing the results, marketers can identify which elements resonate best with their audience and make data-driven decisions to enhance performance. Let's explore the best practices for A/B testing and optimization techniques for landing pages, including key considerations, testing methodologies, and practical tips for achieving meaningful results.

Understanding A/B Testing

Definition: A/B testing, also known as split testing, involves comparing two or more versions of a landing page (A and B) to determine which performs better in terms of a specific metric, such as conversion rate, click-through rate, or engagement. Each version is presented to a segment of the audience, and the results are analyzed to identify the most effective elements.

Importance: A/B testing allows marketers to make informed decisions about landing page design, content, and functionality by testing variations and measuring their impact on user behavior. By systematically testing different elements and analyzing the results, marketers can optimize landing pages for maximum effectiveness and achieve better performance over time.

Key Metrics: When conducting A/B tests, it's essential to define clear objectives and choose relevant metrics to measure success. Common metrics for A/B testing landing pages include conversion rate, click-through rate, bounce rate, time on page, and engagement metrics such as scroll depth or form submissions.

Best Practices for A/B Testing

Start with Clear Objectives: Before conducting A/B tests, clearly define the goals and objectives of the test. Determine which metrics you want to improve and what success looks like for your landing page. Whether it's increasing conversion rates, reducing bounce rates, or improving engagement, having clear objectives will guide your testing strategy.

Test One Variable at a Time: To isolate the impact of individual elements on landing page performance, test one variable at a time. Focus on changing elements such as headlines, call-to-action (CTA) buttons, images, or form fields, and keep all other elements consistent between versions. This approach allows you to accurately measure the impact of each change on user behavior.

<u>Define Hypotheses:</u> Formulate hypotheses based on insights from data, user research, or industry best practices. Clearly state the expected outcome of each test variation and the rationale behind the changes. Hypotheses provide a framework for interpreting test results and guide future optimization efforts.

<u>Segment Your Audience:</u> Segment your audience based on relevant criteria such as demographics, traffic source, or behavior. Test variations on different audience segments to understand how different groups respond to changes and tailor optimizations to specific audience preferences.

<u>Ensure Statistical Significance:</u> Ensure that your A/B tests have a large enough sample size and duration to achieve statistical significance. Use statistical tools or calculators to determine the required sample size based on your desired level of confidence and statistical power. Avoid premature conclusions based on small sample sizes or short test durations.

Practical Tips for A/B Testing

<u>Test High-Impact Elements First:</u> Start by testing elements that are likely to have a significant impact on landing page performance, such as headlines, CTAs, or page layout. These high-impact elements can often produce noticeable improvements in conversion rates and provide quick wins for optimization efforts.

<u>Iterate Based on Insights:</u> Use insights from A/B test results to inform iterative improvements to landing page elements. Analyze test data to understand user behavior, identify patterns or trends, and iteratively optimize elements based on what resonates best with your audience.

<u>Consider User Experience:</u> When designing A/B tests, consider the overall user experience and how changes may impact usability, accessibility, and visual appeal. Test variations on different devices and screen sizes to ensure that landing pages are optimized for all users, regardless of their browsing preferences.

<u>Monitor Results Over Time:</u> Continuously monitor A/B test results over time and track changes in performance metrics. Be prepared to iterate on test variations based on ongoing performance data and adjust testing strategies as needed to achieve desired outcomes.

<u>Document Learnings:</u> Document learnings from A/B tests, including successful variations, failed experiments, and key insights gained from test results. Use this knowledge to inform future testing strategies and build a repository of best practices for landing page optimization.

Advanced Optimization Techniques

<u>Multivariate Testing:</u> In addition to A/B testing, consider conducting multivariate tests to analyze the interaction between multiple elements on landing pages. Multivariate testing allows you to test different combinations of elements simultaneously and identify the most effective combination for maximizing conversion rates.

<u>Personalization:</u> Implement personalized content and messaging on landing pages based on user characteristics, behaviors, or preferences. Use data-driven insights to tailor landing page experiences to individual users, increasing relevance and engagement and driving higher conversion rates.

<u>Behavioral Targeting:</u> Leverage behavioral targeting techniques to deliver targeted content and offers based on user behavior and interactions with your website. Analyze user behavior, such as browsing history, click patterns, or previous interactions, to deliver personalized landing page experiences that resonate with individual users.

<u>Dynamic Content:</u> Implement dynamic content elements on landing pages to deliver personalized messages, offers, or recommendations based on user attributes or behavior. Use dynamic content to create more relevant and engaging landing page experiences that drive higher conversion rates and increase user satisfaction.

A/B testing is a valuable tool for optimizing landing pages and improving conversion rates. By following best practices, testing methodologies, and practical tips, marketers can conduct effective A/B tests that provide meaningful insights and drive continuous improvement. With a data-driven approach to optimization and a focus on delivering engaging and relevant landing page experiences, marketers can achieve better results and maximize the impact of their marketing efforts.

CHAPTER 14: ANALYZING DATA FOR CONTINUOUS IMPROVEMENT

Data analytics plays a crucial role in modern recruitment strategies, allowing organizations to gather insights, measure performance, and optimize campaigns for better results. By leveraging data analytics tools, recruiters can make informed decisions, target the right candidates, and streamline the recruitment process. In this chapter, we will explore the implementation of data analytics tools for recruitment campaigns, including key considerations, best practices, and practical examples of how data analytics can drive success in recruiting.

Understanding Data Analytics in Recruitment

Definition: Data analytics in recruitment involves the collection, analysis, and interpretation of data to gain insights into candidate behavior, recruitment trends, and campaign performance. It encompasses various techniques, including data mining, predictive analytics, and machine learning, to extract valuable information from recruitment data and make data-driven decisions.

<u>Importance:</u> Data analytics enables recruiters to optimize recruitment strategies, improve candidate experiences, and achieve better outcomes. By analyzing recruitment data, recruiters can identify patterns, trends, and opportunities for optimization, leading to more effective hiring processes and higher-quality hires.

<u>Key Metrics:</u> When implementing data analytics in recruitment campaigns, it's essential to define relevant metrics and KPIs to track performance. Common metrics include applicant conversion rate, time-to-hire, cost-per-hire, applicant satisfaction, and candidate quality, among others.

Implementing Data Analytics Tools

<u>Define Objectives and Goals:</u> Start by defining the objectives and goals of your recruitment campaigns. Determine what you want to achieve, whether it's increasing applicant quality, reducing time-to-fill, or improving diversity and inclusion. Align your data analytics efforts with these objectives to ensure that you're measuring the right metrics and optimizing for success.

<u>Choose the Right Tools:</u> Select data analytics tools that align with your recruitment objectives, budget, and technical requirements. There are various tools available, ranging from applicant tracking systems (ATS) and candidate relationship management (CRM) platforms to specialized recruitment analytics software and business intelligence (BI) tools. Choose tools that offer the functionality and features you need to collect, analyze, and visualize recruitment data effectively.

<u>Integrate Data Sources:</u> Integrate data sources to create a centralized repository of recruitment data. This may include data from your ATS, CRM, website analytics, social media

platforms, job boards, and other sources. By consolidating data from multiple sources, recruiters can gain a comprehensive view of candidate interactions, recruitment channels, and campaign performance.

Ensure Data Quality: Ensure data accuracy, completeness, and consistency to generate reliable insights and make informed decisions. Implement data validation processes, standardize data formats, and address data quality issues proactively to maintain the integrity of your recruitment data. Regularly audit and clean your data to identify and correct errors or discrepancies.

Compliance and Privacy: Ensure compliance with data protection regulations, such as GDPR or CCPA, when collecting and processing recruitment data. Implement data privacy measures to protect candidate information and ensure that data analytics practices adhere to legal and ethical standards. Obtain consent from candidates before collecting and using their data for analytics purposes and provide transparency about how their data will be used.

Leveraging Data Analytics for Recruitment

Candidate Sourcing and Acquisition: Use data analytics to identify the most effective candidate sourcing channels and optimize recruitment advertising strategies. Analyze data on applicant sources, conversion rates, and cost-per-acquisition to determine which channels are driving the highest-quality candidates and allocate resources accordingly.

Candidate Experience Optimization: Analyze candidate journey data to identify pain points, bottlenecks, and areas for improvement in the recruitment process. Use data analytics to optimize the candidate experience at every touchpoint, from job search and application to interview and onboarding, to attract and retain top talent. Look for ghost points where candidates do not show up for new hire process appointments. Ghost points equal candidate journey failure.

Performance Monitoring and Optimization: Monitor recruitment campaign performance in real-time and track key metrics to assess effectiveness and identify areas for optimization. Use data analytics to analyze campaign performance trends, compare results against benchmarks, and identify opportunities for improvement.

Predictive Analytics and Forecasting: Use predictive analytics models to forecast future recruitment trends, anticipate hiring needs, and proactively address talent gaps. Analyze historical recruitment data to identify patterns and predict future hiring demand, enabling recruiters to develop proactive talent acquisition strategies and stay ahead of workforce planning challenges.

Diversity and Inclusion: Use data analytics to track diversity and inclusion metrics and measure progress towards diversity goals. Analyze data on candidate demographics, hiring outcomes, and representation in the workforce to identify areas for improvement and implement strategies to promote diversity and inclusion in recruitment.

Data analytics is a powerful tool for optimizing recruitment campaigns, improving candidate experiences, and driving better hiring outcomes. By implementing data analytics tools, recruiters can gain valuable insights into candidate behavior, recruitment trends, and campaign performance, enabling them to make informed decisions and achieve their recruitment objectives. With the right data analytics strategies, recruiters can attract top talent, streamline the hiring process, and build a strong and diverse workforce to support organizational success.

Defining Key Performance Indicators and Tracking in Recruitment Campaigns

Key Performance Indicators (KPIs) are critical metrics that organizations use to measure the effectiveness and success of their recruitment campaigns. By defining and tracking KPIs, recruiters can assess the performance of their efforts, identify areas for improvement, and make data-driven decisions to optimize recruitment strategies. Let's explore the process of defining KPIs and tracking them in recruitment campaigns, including key considerations, common KPIs, and best practices for effective measurement and analysis.

Understanding Key Performance Indicators (KPIs) in Recruitment

Definition: Key Performance Indicators (KPIs) are quantifiable metrics used to evaluate the performance and success of recruitment campaigns. KPIs provide valuable insights into various aspects of the recruitment process, including candidate sourcing, applicant quality, time-to-fill, cost-per-hire, and candidate experience.

Importance: KPIs enable recruiters to measure progress towards recruitment goals, identify strengths and weaknesses in their strategies, and make informed decisions to optimize performance. By tracking KPIs, recruiters can ensure that their recruitment efforts align with organizational objectives and contribute to overall business success.

Key Considerations: When defining KPIs for recruitment campaigns, it's essential to consider the specific goals and objectives of the organization, the target audience, and the desired outcomes of the recruitment process. KPIs should be relevant, measurable, achievable, and aligned with business priorities to provide meaningful insights and drive actionable results.

Common Key Performance Indicators (KPIs) in Recruitment

Applicant Sourcing Metrics:

Source of Hire: The channels or methods through which candidates were sourced or recruited, such as job boards, social media, employee referrals, or career fairs.

Cost-per-Hire: The total cost incurred to recruit and hire a candidate, including expenses related to advertising, sourcing, recruiting, and onboarding.

Time-to-Fill: The average time it takes to fill open positions from the initiation of the recruitment process to the acceptance of a job offer by a candidate.

Applicant Quality: The quality of candidates attracted to open positions, measured based on criteria such as qualifications, skills, experience, and fit with organizational culture.

Candidate Engagement Metrics:

Application Completion Rate: The percentage of candidates who successfully complete the application process after initiating an application.

Candidate Response Rate: The percentage of candidates who respond to outreach or communication from recruiters, such as emails, phone calls, or messages.

Candidate Experience Score: The rating or feedback provided by candidates on their experience with the recruitment process, including interactions with recruiters, the application process, and interview experiences.

Hiring Process Metrics:

Offer Acceptance Rate: The percentage of candidates who accept job offers after receiving an offer of employment from the organization.

Offer Decline Rate: The percentage of candidates who decline job offers after receiving an offer of employment from the organization.

Onboarding Completion Rate: The percentage of new hires who complete the onboarding process and become fully integrated into the organization.

Best Practices for Tracking KPIs in Recruitment Campaigns

Define Clear Objectives: Start by defining clear objectives and goals for your recruitment campaigns. Determine what you want to achieve, whether it's increasing applicant quality, reducing time-to-fill, or improving candidate experience. Align your KPIs with these objectives to ensure that you're measuring the right metrics and tracking progress towards your goals.

Select Relevant Metrics: Choose KPIs that are relevant to your recruitment objectives and provide meaningful insights into the performance of your campaigns. Focus on metrics that directly impact recruitment outcomes, such as applicant sourcing, candidate engagement, and hiring process efficiency.

Establish Baseline Measurements: Establish baseline measurements for your KPIs to provide context and benchmark performance over time. Collect historical data on key metrics to understand current performance levels and identify trends or patterns that may impact future outcomes.

Implement Data Collection Mechanisms: Implement data collection mechanisms to track KPIs effectively. Utilize recruitment software, applicant tracking systems (ATS), and other tools to capture and store recruitment data, including applicant information, sourcing channels, and hiring process metrics.

Regularly Monitor and Analyze Data: Regularly monitor and analyze KPI data to track performance, identify trends, and detect anomalies. Use data visualization tools, dashboards, and reports to visualize KPIs and communicate insights to stakeholders effectively.

Conduct Ongoing Optimization: Use KPI data to identify areas for optimization and make data-driven decisions to improve recruitment performance. Experiment with different strategies, tactics, and approaches based on KPI insights and iterate on recruitment campaigns to achieve better results.

Defining and tracking key performance indicators (KPIs)

is essential for evaluating the effectiveness and success of recruitment campaigns. By selecting relevant metrics, establishing baseline measurements, implementing data collection mechanisms, and regularly monitoring and analyzing data, recruiters can gain valuable insights into recruitment performance and make data-driven decisions to optimize their strategies. With a focus on continuous improvement and alignment with organizational objectives, tracking KPIs can help recruiters achieve better recruitment outcomes, attract top talent, and build a strong and diverse workforce for the future.

Utilizing Iterative Improvement Based on Data Insights in Fire and Police Recruiting

In the dynamic landscape of fire and police recruiting, the ability to adapt and evolve recruitment strategies based on data insights is crucial for success. By leveraging data-driven approaches and adopting iterative improvement methodologies, fire and police departments can enhance their recruitment efforts, attract qualified candidates, and build stronger, more diverse teams. Let's explore the importance of iterative improvement based on data insights in fire and police recruiting, including key principles, best practices, and practical examples of how departments can leverage data to optimize their recruitment strategies.

Understanding Iterative Improvement in Recruitment

Definition: Iterative improvement, also known as continuous improvement or agile methodology, involves making incremental changes to recruitment strategies based on data insights and feedback. Rather than relying on static or one-size-fits-all approaches, iterative improvement emphasizes experimentation, learning, and adaptation to achieve better results over time.

Importance: In the fast-paced and competitive environment of fire and police recruiting, iterative improvement allows departments to respond quickly to changing conditions, identify opportunities for optimization, and make data-driven decisions to enhance recruitment effectiveness. By continuously refining recruitment strategies based on real-time data insights, departments can stay ahead of the curve and attract top talent to serve and protect their communities effectively.

Key Principles: Iterative improvement in recruitment is guided by several key principles, including:

Data-Driven Decision-Making: Making decisions based on data insights and analytics rather than assumptions or intuition.

Continuous Feedback Loops: Establishing mechanisms for collecting feedback from candidates, recruiters, and stakeholders to inform ongoing improvements.

Experimentation and Innovation: Encouraging experimentation and innovation to test new ideas, strategies, and approaches and identify what works best.

Rapid Iteration: Iterating quickly on recruitment strategies based on feedback and performance data to achieve incremental improvements over time.

Adaptability and Flexibility: Remaining flexible and adaptable in response to changing recruitment trends, candidate preferences, and organizational needs.

Implementing Iterative Improvement in Fire and Police Recruiting

Define Clear Objectives: Start by defining clear objectives and goals for your recruitment efforts, such as increasing applicant quality, reducing time-to-hire, or improving diversity and inclusion. Align your objectives with organizational priorities and establish key performance indicators (KPIs) to measure progress toward your goals.

Collect and Analyze Data: Collect and analyze data from various sources, including applicant tracking systems (ATS), recruitment software, website analytics, and candidate feedback surveys. Use data analytics tools and techniques to gain insights into candidate behavior, recruitment trends, and campaign performance.

Identify Areas for Improvement: Use data insights to identify areas for improvement in your recruitment strategies, such as ineffective sourcing channels, low applicant conversion rates, or high dropout rates in the hiring process. Look for patterns, trends, and opportunities for optimization based on data analysis.

Experiment with Different Strategies: Experiment with different recruitment strategies, tactics, and approaches to test hypotheses and validate assumptions. Try new sourcing channels, messaging techniques, or candidate engagement initiatives and measure their impact on recruitment outcomes.

Measure and Evaluate Results: Measure the results of your recruitment experiments and initiatives against established KPIs to assess their effectiveness. Evaluate the impact of changes on recruitment performance metrics such as applicant quality, time-to-hire, and candidate satisfaction.

Adapt and Iterate Based on Feedback: Use feedback from candidates, recruiters, and stakeholders to inform iterative improvements to your recruitment strategies. Incorporate feedback into your decision-making process and adjust recruitment tactics accordingly to address concerns or areas for improvement.

Best Practices for Iterative Improvement in Fire and Police Recruiting

Establish a Culture of Continuous Improvement: Foster a culture of continuous improvement within your fire or police department, where experimentation, learning, and adaptation are encouraged and rewarded. Create opportunities for knowledge sharing, collaboration, and innovation among recruiters and stakeholders.

Invest in Data Analytics Capabilities: Invest in data analytics tools, technologies, and training to build data-driven capabilities within your recruitment team. Equip recruiters with the skills and resources they need to collect, analyze, and interpret recruitment data effectively.

Embrace Agile Methodologies: Embrace agile methodologies such as Scrum or Kanban to facilitate iterative improvement in recruitment. Break down recruitment initiatives into smaller, manageable tasks or experiments, and iterate on them in short, focused cycles.

Monitor Recruitment Trends and Best Practices: Stay informed about emerging trends, best practices, and innovations in fire and police recruiting. Attend industry conferences, workshops, and webinars, and engage with professional networks to learn from peers and stay ahead of the curve.

<u>Celebrate Successes and Learn from Failures:</u> Celebrate successes and milestones achieved through iterative improvement efforts, and share lessons learned from both successes and failures. Encourage a culture of experimentation and learning from mistakes to drive continuous improvement in recruitment.

Iterative improvement based on data insights is essential for driving success in fire and police recruiting. By adopting a data-driven approach, embracing agile methodologies, and fostering a culture of continuous improvement, fire and police departments can optimize their recruitment strategies, attract qualified candidates, and build stronger, more resilient teams to serve and protect their communities effectively.

With a commitment to learning, experimentation, and adaptation, fire and police recruiters can stay ahead of the curve and achieve better recruitment outcomes in an ever-evolving landscape.

CHAPTER 15: IDENTIFYING AND UNDERSTANDING THE RECRUITMENT JOURNEY FOR POTENTIAL MEMBERS OF THE FIRE & POLICE SERVICE

Recruiting individuals into the fire and police services is a multifaceted process that involves understanding the journey potential candidates undertake from initial awareness to becoming fully-fledged members of these essential public safety organizations. By gaining insights into the recruitment journey, fire and police departments can tailor their strategies to effectively engage and attract qualified candidates. Let's delve into the recruitment journey for potential members of the fire and police service, exploring key stages, challenges, and strategies for successful recruitment.

Awareness and Consideration Stage

Initial Awareness: The recruitment journey often begins with potential candidates becoming aware of career opportunities in the fire and police services. This awareness can be triggered by various factors, including personal interest, recommendations from friends or family, or exposure to recruitment marketing efforts such as job postings, social media campaigns, or community outreach events.

Information Gathering: Once aware of career opportunities, potential candidates typically engage in information gathering to learn more about the requirements, responsibilities, and benefits of working in the fire or police service. They may research department websites, attend recruitment events, speak with current or former members of the service, or seek guidance from career counselors or mentors.

Consideration: As candidates gather information, they begin to consider whether a career in the fire or police service aligns with their interests, skills, and values. They weigh factors such as job stability, salary, work-life balance, and opportunities for advancement, as well as the intrinsic rewards of serving their community and making a difference in people's lives.

The awareness and consideration stage can be thought of as a dating process. It would seem very strange to walk up to a potential partner that you have never met before and ask them to marry you. But we do this every time we ask a potential recruit to "apply now". We should design our processes so that we take potential recruits through a guided awareness/ information gathering/consideration process so that they do not feel pressured or question their ability to be successful. Inform potential candidates about the career, invite them to informal information sessions and then provide them the information they need to consider the career. Just like a first date over coffee, the recruiting effort should utilize a systematic approach to allow the recruit to get to know us a little more.

Application and Assessment Stage

Application Submission: Candidates who decide to pursue a career in the fire or police service typically submit applications to the respective departments. This involves completing application forms, providing relevant documentation such as resumes, transcripts, and certifications, and possibly undergoing preliminary screening processes to ensure eligibility.

Assessment Process: Upon receiving applications, fire and police departments may conduct various assessments to evaluate candidates' suitability for the role. This may include written examinations, physical fitness tests, psychological evaluations, background checks, and interviews to assess candidates' skills, abilities, and suitability for the demands of the job. The assessment process includes ghost points where candidates will not show up for scheduled assessments. High ghost points are indicative of not providing enough information and not communicating enough with the candidate. Both of these can be improved through communication automation and artificial intelligence solutions.

Selection Criteria: Departments establish specific selection criteria based on the requirements of the role and the needs of the organization. These criteria may vary depending on factors such as jurisdictional regulations, departmental policies, and the nature of the position being filled, whether it's a firefighter, police officer, dispatcher, or other roles within the organization.

Engagement and Decision-Making Stage

Engagement with Recruiters: Throughout the application and assessment process, candidates engage with recruiters, hiring managers, and departmental representatives who provide guidance, answer questions, and facilitate the recruitment journey. Effective communication and support from recruiters can significantly impact candidates' perceptions of the department and their overall experience.

Decision-Making: After completing assessments and engaging with recruiters, candidates reach a decision point where they must decide whether to accept a job offer from the fire or police department. This decision is influenced by various factors, including the candidate's personal preferences, career goals, the department's reputation, and the terms and conditions of employment offered by the organization.

Offer Acceptance: Candidates who receive job offers may choose to accept, decline, or negotiate the terms of the offer based on their circumstances and preferences. Factors such as salary, benefits, location, career advancement opportunities, and organizational culture may influence candidates' decisions to accept or decline offers.

Onboarding and Integration Stage

Onboarding Process: Upon accepting a job offer, recruits undergo an onboarding process to familiarize themselves with the department, its policies, procedures, and organizational culture. This may involve orientation sessions, training programs, mentorship initiatives, and introductions to colleagues and supervisors to facilitate a smooth transition into the organization.

Understanding the recruitment journey for potential members of the fire and police service is essential for designing effective recruitment strategies and attracting qualified candidates to these critical public safety organizations. By recognizing the key stages, challenges, and decision points in the recruitment journey, fire and police departments can tailor their efforts to engage, attract, and retain top talent, ensuring the continued safety and well-being of the communities they serve. Through ongoing assessment, adaptation, and innovation, fire and police departments can build stronger, more resilient teams to address the evolving challenges of public safety in the 21st century.

Recognizing Failure Points in the Recruiting Process and Addressing Candidate Ghosting and No-Show Issues

The recruiting process is not without its challenges, and one of the most frustrating experiences for recruiters is when candidates ghost or fail to show up for scheduled interviews or assessments. Candidate ghosting and no-shows can significantly disrupt recruitment efforts, waste valuable time and resources, and create inefficiencies in the hiring process. Let's explore the various failure points in the recruiting process that can lead to candidate ghosting and no-shows, as well as strategies and best practices for addressing these issues effectively.

Understanding Candidate Ghosting and No-Show Events

<u>Candidate Ghosting:</u> Candidate ghosting refers to the

phenomenon where candidates abruptly cease communication or fail to respond to outreach from recruiters or hiring managers. This can occur at any stage of the recruitment process, from initial contact to post-offer negotiations, and can leave recruiters in the dark about the candidate's intentions or reasons for disengagement.

No-Show Events: No-show events occur when candidates fail to attend scheduled interviews, assessments, or other recruitment-related appointments without prior notice or explanation. No-shows can disrupt recruitment schedules, inconvenience recruiters and hiring teams, and reflect poorly on the candidate's reliability and professionalism.

Impact on Recruitment: Candidate ghosting and no-show events can have significant consequences for the recruitment process, including delays in filling open positions, increased time-to-fill, decreased candidate engagement and satisfaction, and negative impacts on employer branding and reputation. These issues can also create additional work for recruiters and hiring teams, who must reschedule appointments, follow up with candidates, and potentially restart the recruitment process from scratch.

Identifying Failure Points in the Recruiting Process

Lack of Communication: Poor communication practices, such as delayed responses, unclear instructions, or inconsistent messaging, can contribute to candidate ghosting and no-show events. Candidates may feel frustrated or disengaged if they perceive a lack of communication or transparency from recruiters, leading them to disengage from the recruitment process altogether.

<u>Lengthy and Complex Processes:</u> Lengthy or overly complex recruitment processes can deter candidates from completing their applications or attending scheduled interviews. Excessive paperwork, redundant assessments, or lengthy wait times between interview rounds can lead to candidate fatigue and disinterest, increasing the likelihood of ghosting or no-show events.

<u>Poor Candidate Experience:</u> A negative candidate experience, characterized by impersonal interactions, unprofessional behavior, or lack of engagement from recruiters, can drive candidates to disengage from the recruitment process. Candidates who feel undervalued or disrespected are more likely to ghost or no-show on scheduled appointments.

<u>Lack of Clarity and Expectations:</u> Unclear expectations or requirements for the role, such as ambiguous job descriptions, unrealistic qualifications, or conflicting information about the recruitment process, can confuse candidates and lead to uncertainty or frustration. Candidates may lose interest or confidence in the opportunity if they are unsure about what is expected of them or how to proceed.

Addressing Candidate Ghosting and No-Show Events

<u>Improve Communication Practices:</u> Enhance communication practices throughout the recruitment process to keep candidates informed, engaged, and motivated. Provide timely updates, clear instructions, and transparent feedback to candidates at every stage, and encourage open dialogue and two-way communication to address any concerns or questions they may have.

Streamline the Recruitment Process: Streamline the recruitment process to minimize unnecessary steps, reduce bureaucratic barriers, and expedite decision-making. Simplify application procedures, consolidate interview rounds, and leverage technology solutions such as applicant tracking systems (ATS) or scheduling tools to automate administrative tasks and streamline communication with candidates.

Enhance the Candidate Experience: Prioritize the candidate experience by creating personalized, engaging, and memorable interactions throughout the recruitment journey. Tailor recruitment messages and materials to align with candidates' interests, values, and career goals, and provide opportunities for candidates to showcase their skills and potential contributions to the organization.

Set Clear Expectations: Establish clear expectations and guidelines for candidates regarding the recruitment process, including timelines, requirements, and next steps. Provide detailed job descriptions, realistic expectations about the selection process, and transparent information about the organization's culture, values, and expectations for new hires.

Implement Confirmation and Reminder Systems: Implement confirmation and reminder systems to reduce the risk of candidate no-show events. Send automated email or text reminders to candidates prior to scheduled interviews or assessments, confirming the date, time, location, and any additional instructions or materials required for the appointment.

Reach Out to Candidate: Many times candidates have life issues that derail good intentions. Sickness, lack of transportation, or a multitude of factors could have affected the candidate's ability to show up. Reach out with texts, emails, and voice mails to let the candidate know you understand if life factors resulted in a no-show and you would like to give them a second chance. Gen Z candidates are too embarrassed to contact you when life gets in the way of an appointment. Allowing the candidate to have 1 ghost event with no penalty can help increase your success rate and let the candidate know you are an understanding organization.

Develop Contingency Plans: Develop contingency plans to mitigate the impact of candidate ghosting and no-show events on recruitment schedules and outcomes. Establish backup candidates, alternative interview dates, or flexible assessment options to accommodate unexpected changes or cancellations and minimize disruptions to the recruitment process.

Monitoring and Continuous Improvement

Track and Analyze Metrics: Track and analyze recruitment metrics related to candidate engagement, communication effectiveness, and no-show rates to identify trends, patterns, and areas for improvement. Monitor key performance indicators (KPIs) such as time-to-fill, applicant conversion rates, and candidate satisfaction scores to assess the impact of interventions and adjustments.

Solicit Feedback from Candidates: Solicit feedback from candidates about their recruitment experience to gain insights into their perceptions, preferences, and pain points. Conduct post-application surveys, exit interviews, or follow-up conversations with candidates to gather feedback about their interactions with recruiters, the clarity of recruitment processes, and overall satisfaction with the experience.

Iterate and Adapt: Continuously iterate and adapt recruitment strategies based on feedback, data insights, and evolving candidate expectations. Experiment with new approaches, test hypotheses, and monitor outcomes to identify what works best for attracting, engaging, and retaining top talent in the fire and police services. If you are experiencing lackluster recruiting efforts the problem lies with your process. Blaming poor recruiting on the behaviors of Gen Z recruits will just allow your recruiting to continue to suffer. Researching failure points and trying different solutions will help you unlock hidden potential.

Candidate ghosting and no-show events present significant challenges for recruiters in the fire and police services, but with proactive measures and strategic interventions, these issues can be addressed effectively. By identifying failure points in the recruitment process, improving communication practices, enhancing the candidate experience, and implementing contingency plans, fire and police departments can minimize the impact of candidate ghosting and no-show events on recruitment outcomes and build stronger, more resilient teams to serve and protect their communities. Through ongoing monitoring, feedback collection, and continuous improvement efforts, recruiters can optimize the recruitment process and ensure a positive experience for candidates while meeting the staffing needs of their organizations.

Utilizing Automatic Text and Email Messaging and Artificial Intelligence to Improve the Recruitment Candidate Journey and Reduce Ghosting

In today's fast-paced digital world, leveraging technology to enhance the recruitment candidate journey is essential for fire and police departments aiming to attract and retain top talent. Automatic text and email messaging, powered by artificial intelligence (AI), offer innovative solutions to streamline communication, personalize interactions, and reduce candidate ghosting throughout the recruitment process. Let's explore the benefits of utilizing automatic text and email messaging and AI in recruitment, practical applications for improving the candidate journey, and strategies for reducing ghosting to ensure a positive and efficient recruitment experience.

The Role of Technology in Recruitment

<u>Evolution of Recruitment Technology:</u> Over the years, recruitment technology has evolved significantly, from traditional methods such as newspaper advertisements and job fairs to digital platforms, applicant tracking systems (ATS), and AI-powered solutions. These advancements have revolutionized the way organizations attract, engage, and hire candidates, enabling more efficient and effective recruitment processes.

<u>Importance of Communication in Recruitment:</u> Communication plays a critical role in the recruitment candidate journey, from initial engagement to post-offer negotiations. Clear, timely, and personalized communication can enhance the candidate experience, build trust and rapport, and differentiate organizations as employers of choice. Conversely, poor communication practices can lead to candidate dissatisfaction, disengagement, and ultimately, ghosting.

Leveraging Automatic Text and Email Messaging

<u>Benefits of Automatic Messaging:</u> Automatic text and email messaging offer several advantages for recruitment, including:

<u>Instant Communication:</u> Automatic messaging allows

recruiters to reach candidates instantly, providing timely updates, reminders, and notifications throughout the recruitment process.

Personalization: AI-powered algorithms can personalize messaging based on candidate preferences, behavior, and interaction history, creating a more tailored and engaging experience for candidates.

Efficiency: Automatic messaging streamlines communication workflows, reducing manual effort and administrative burden for recruiters and hiring teams.

Accessibility: Text and email messaging are accessible to candidates across devices and platforms, ensuring seamless communication regardless of location or time zone.

Practical Applications

Application Acknowledgment: Automatically send confirmation messages to candidates upon receiving their applications, acknowledging receipt and providing information about the next steps in the recruitment process.

Interview Reminders: Send automated reminders to candidates before scheduled interviews, including details such as date, time, location, and any preparation materials or instructions.

Status Updates: Provide regular updates to candidates about the status of their application, including progress through the selection process, interview outcomes, and next steps.

Feedback Requests: Solicit feedback from candidates about their recruitment experience through automated surveys or feedback forms, capturing valuable insights to improve future processes.

Harnessing Artificial Intelligence in Recruitment

<u>Role of AI in Recruitment:</u> AI technology is transforming the recruitment landscape, enabling organizations to automate repetitive tasks, analyze vast amounts of data, and make data-driven decisions to optimize recruitment strategies. AI-powered solutions can enhance candidate sourcing, screening, engagement, and retention, improving recruitment outcomes and efficiency.

Applications of AI in Recruitment:

<u>Candidate Sourcing:</u> AI algorithms can analyze candidate profiles and resumes to identify potential matches for open positions, helping recruiters source candidates more effectively and efficiently.

<u>Resume Screening:</u> AI-powered screening tools can automatically analyze resumes, identify relevant keywords and qualifications, and rank candidates based on their fit for the role, saving time and reducing bias in the selection process.

<u>Chatbots:</u> AI-driven chatbots can engage with candidates in real-time, answering questions, providing information about job opportunities, and guiding candidates through the application process, even outside of business hours.

<u>Predictive Analytics:</u> AI algorithms can analyze recruitment data to identify patterns, trends, and correlations that predict candidate behavior and likelihood of success, enabling recruiters to make more informed decisions about candidate selection and retention.

Strategies for Reducing Candidate Ghosting

Personalized Engagement: Leverage AI and automatic messaging to personalize communication with candidates, addressing their individual needs, preferences, and concerns. Tailor messages to resonate with candidates' interests, motivations, and career aspirations, fostering a stronger connection and reducing the likelihood of ghosting.

Transparent Communication: Maintain transparency throughout the recruitment process, providing candidates with clear expectations, timelines, and feedback. Communicate openly about the organization's values, culture, and expectations for new hires, setting the stage for a positive and mutually beneficial relationship.

Proactive Outreach: Use automatic messaging and AI-driven chatbots to proactively engage with candidates at key touchpoints in the recruitment journey. Reach out to candidates to check in on their progress, offer assistance or support, and address any concerns or questions they may have, demonstrating your commitment to their success.

Automated Reminders: Send automated reminders to candidates about upcoming interviews, assessments, or deadlines, reducing the risk of no-show events and ensuring that candidates remain engaged and informed throughout the process.

Feedback Collection: Use automated surveys or feedback forms to collect input from candidates about their recruitment experience, including their satisfaction levels, pain points, and suggestions for improvement. Analyze feedback data to identify areas for optimization and implement changes to enhance the candidate journey.

Automatic text and email messaging, combined with artificial intelligence, offer powerful tools for enhancing the recruitment candidate journey and reducing ghosting in the fire and police services. By leveraging technology to personalize communication, streamline processes, and proactively engage with candidates, fire and police departments can create a more positive and efficient recruitment experience for candidates while achieving better outcomes for their organizations. Through continuous innovation, experimentation, and adaptation, recruiters can harness the potential of automatic messaging and AI to attract, engage, and retain top talent in the public safety sector, ensuring the safety and well-being of communities for years to come.

CHAPTER 16: RECAP OF KEY STRATEGIES AND TECHNIQUES DISCUSSED IN THE BOOK

Navigating Challenges and Maximizing Opportunities in Police and Fire Recruiting

In the competitive landscape of police and fire recruiting, agencies face a myriad of challenges in attracting and retaining qualified personnel. From demographic shifts to evolving candidate expectations, agencies must navigate a complex landscape to effectively fill crucial positions. In this chapter, we'll recap the current challenges in police and fire recruiting and explore strategic approaches to overcome them, including understanding demographic targeting, crafting compelling messages, leveraging search and social media ads, exploring programmatic and IP targeting, creating effective landing pages, and using data analytics for highly effective recruiting.

Current Challenges in Police and Fire Recruiting

Demographic Shifts: Police and fire agencies are facing demographic shifts, including an aging workforce and changing population dynamics. Recruiting efforts must adapt to attract candidates from diverse age groups and backgrounds to ensure a sustainable pipeline of talent.

Competitive Job Market: The competitive job market poses challenges for police and fire recruiting, with candidates having more options and opportunities than ever before. Agencies must differentiate themselves as employers of choice and offer competitive compensation, benefits, and career advancement opportunities to attract top talent.

Evolving Candidate Expectations: Candidates have increasingly high expectations when it comes to the recruitment process, seeking transparency, flexibility, and a positive candidate experience. Agencies must prioritize clear communication, streamlined processes, and personalized interactions to meet these expectations and effectively engage candidates.

Understanding Demographic Targeting

Tailoring Recruitment Efforts: Demographic targeting allows police and fire agencies to tailor their recruitment efforts to specific demographic groups, such as age, gender, education level, and geographic location. By understanding the unique preferences and motivations of different demographics, agencies can craft targeted messages and outreach strategies to effectively reach and engage potential candidates.

Inclusive Recruitment Practices: Demographic targeting also enables agencies to implement more inclusive recruitment practices, ensuring that their messaging and outreach efforts resonate with candidates from diverse backgrounds and experiences. By actively seeking out and engaging with underrepresented groups, agencies can foster diversity and inclusion within their ranks and better reflect the communities they serve.

Crafting Compelling Messages

Storytelling and Branding: Crafting compelling messages is essential to capture the attention and interest of potential candidates. Agencies can leverage storytelling and branding techniques to showcase their mission, values, and impact, creating an emotional connection with candidates and inspiring them to join the force.

Highlighting Benefits and Opportunities: Messages should highlight the benefits and opportunities of a career in law enforcement or firefighting, including job security, career advancement, training programs, and opportunities to make a difference in the community. By emphasizing the rewards and fulfillment of public service, agencies can attract candidates who are passionate about making a positive impact.

Leveraging Search Ads for Recruitment

Targeted Advertising: Search ads allow police and fire agencies to target specific keywords and phrases related to recruitment, ensuring that their ads are shown to candidates actively searching for career opportunities in public safety. By bidding on relevant keywords and optimizing ad content, agencies can increase their visibility and attract qualified candidates to their recruitment website or landing pages.

Geographic Targeting: Geographic targeting enables agencies to focus their search ads on specific geographic areas, such as cities, counties, or regions, where they have recruitment needs. By targeting ads to locations with high demand for public safety personnel, agencies can maximize their reach and impact in key markets.

Harnessing Social Media Ads for Recruitment

Audience Segmentation: Social media ads offer advanced audience segmentation capabilities, allowing police and fire agencies to target ads based on demographic, psychographic, and behavioral factors. Agencies can create custom audience segments and deliver tailored messages to specific groups of candidates, increasing the relevance and effectiveness of their recruitment efforts.

Visual Storytelling: Social media ads provide opportunities for visual storytelling, allowing agencies to showcase their culture, values, and impact through compelling images and videos. By leveraging visual content, agencies can capture the attention of candidates scrolling through their social media feeds and effectively communicate their message memorably and engagingly.

Exploring Programmatic Advertising

Automated Campaign Management: Programmatic advertising enables police and fire agencies to automate the management of their recruitment campaigns, including ad placement, targeting, and optimization. By leveraging data-driven algorithms and real-time bidding strategies, agencies can maximize the efficiency and effectiveness of their advertising efforts while minimizing manual effort and resources.

Behavioral Targeting: Programmatic advertising allows agencies to target ads based on user behavior and interests, delivering personalized messages to candidates who are most likely to be interested in public safety careers. By analyzing online behavior and engagement metrics, agencies can identify and reach candidates who exhibit relevant traits and characteristics, increasing the likelihood of conversion and engagement.

Using Precision Targeting with IP Targeting

Hyper-Local Targeting: IP targeting enables police and fire agencies to target ads to specific IP addresses or geographic locations, such as neighborhoods, zip codes, or even individual households. By leveraging IP targeting, agencies can deliver highly targeted messages to candidates in their local community, increasing relevance and engagement.

Event-Based Targeting: IP targeting can also be used to target ads to specific events or locations where recruitment opportunities are present, such as job fairs, community events, or college campuses. By identifying IP addresses associated with these events, agencies can reach candidates who are actively seeking career opportunities in public safety and are more likely to be receptive to recruitment messages.

Creating Effective Landing Pages

Clear Call-to-Action: Effective landing pages should have a clear call-to-action (CTA) that prompts visitors to take the desired action, such as submitting an application or requesting more information. The CTA should be prominently displayed and visually appealing, encouraging visitors to engage with the page and take the next step in the recruitment process.

Mobile Optimization: Landing pages should be optimized for mobile devices, ensuring that they load quickly and display properly on smartphones and tablets. With an increasing number of candidates using mobile devices to browse the internet, mobile optimization is essential to provide a seamless and user-friendly experience for visitors.

Using Data Analytics for Highly Effective Recruiting

Performance Tracking: Data analytics allows police and fire agencies to track the performance of their recruitment campaigns and measure key metrics such as website traffic, conversion rates, and applicant demographics. By analyzing these metrics, agencies can gain valuable insights into the effectiveness of their strategies and make data-driven decisions to optimize their recruiting efforts.

Audience Insights: Data analytics provides agencies with valuable audience insights, including demographic information, online behavior, and engagement patterns. By understanding their target audience, agencies can tailor their messaging and outreach strategies to better resonate with candidates and improve recruitment outcomes.

Continuous Improvement: Data analytics enables agencies to continuously monitor and refine their recruitment strategies based on real-time feedback and performance data. By identifying areas for improvement and implementing iterative changes, agencies can maximize the effectiveness of their recruiting efforts and achieve better results over time.

In the rapidly evolving landscape of police and fire

recruiting, agencies must adapt to overcome current challenges and maximize opportunities for success. By understanding demographic targeting, crafting compelling messages, leveraging search and social media ads, exploring programmatic and IP targeting, creating effective landing pages, and using data analytics for highly effective recruiting, agencies can attract and retain top talent to serve and protect their communities. Through strategic planning, innovative tactics, and continuous improvement, police and fire agencies can build strong, diverse, and resilient teams capable of meeting the evolving needs of their communities now and in the future.

Embracing Digital Marketing Tactics to Enhance Recruitment Efforts In Public Safety Agencies

In today's digital age, public safety agencies face increasing challenges in recruiting and retaining qualified personnel to serve and protect their communities. To address these challenges, it's crucial for public safety agencies to embrace digital marketing tactics as a strategic approach to attract, engage, and retain top talent. Let's explore the importance of digital marketing in recruitment efforts for public safety agencies, the benefits it offers, and practical strategies for implementation.

The Importance of Digital Marketing in Recruitment

Changing Recruitment Landscape: The recruitment landscape for public safety agencies has evolved significantly in recent years, driven by technological advancements, demographic shifts, and changing candidate preferences. Traditional recruitment methods such as job fairs and print advertisements are no longer sufficient to reach and engage modern candidates effectively.

Digital Reach and Engagement: Digital marketing offers public safety agencies unparalleled reach and engagement with potential candidates. Through online platforms such as social media, search engines, and job boards, agencies can target specific demographics, personalize messaging, and foster meaningful connections with candidates throughout the recruitment journey.

Competitive Advantage: Embracing digital marketing tactics gives public safety agencies a competitive advantage in the recruitment market. By leveraging innovative strategies such as demographic targeting, storytelling messaging, and data analytics, agencies can differentiate themselves as employers of choice and attract top talent in a competitive landscape.

Benefits of Digital Marketing in Recruitment Efforts

Targeted Recruitment: Digital marketing allows public safety agencies to target specific demographics, geographic locations, and candidate profiles with precision. By identifying and reaching out to the most relevant audiences, agencies can maximize the effectiveness of their recruitment efforts and increase the likelihood of attracting qualified candidates.

Enhanced Brand Visibility: Digital marketing helps public safety agencies enhance their brand visibility and awareness among potential candidates. Through compelling content, engaging visuals, and strategic messaging, agencies can showcase their mission, values, and culture, creating a compelling employer brand that resonates with candidates.

Cost-Effective Solutions: Compared to traditional recruitment methods, digital marketing offers cost-effective solutions for public safety agencies. Platforms such as social media and search engines allow agencies to reach a large audience at a fraction of the cost of traditional advertising channels, maximizing return on investment (ROI) and optimizing recruitment budgets.

Data-Driven Insights: Digital marketing provides public safety agencies with valuable data-driven insights into candidate behavior, preferences, and engagement metrics. By analyzing recruitment analytics, agencies can gain a deeper understanding of their target audience, identify trends and patterns, and optimize their recruitment strategies for better results.

Practical Strategies for Implementing Digital Marketing Tactics

Define Recruitment Objectives: Start by defining clear recruitment objectives and goals for your public safety agency. Determine the positions you need to fill, the target demographics you want to reach, and the key performance indicators (KPIs) you will use to measure success.

Identify Target Audiences: Use demographic targeting tools to identify and reach specific target audiences for your recruitment campaigns. Consider factors such as age, location, education level, and interests to tailor your messaging and content to resonate with the right candidates.

Craft Compelling Messaging: Develop compelling messaging that highlights the unique value proposition of working for your public safety agency. Emphasize factors such as career advancement opportunities, competitive salaries, benefits, and the opportunity to make a meaningful difference in the community.

Utilize story-based Techniques: Apply story-based messaging principles to create engaging narratives that resonate with potential candidates. Frame your recruitment messaging around a compelling storyline that showcases the challenges, rewards, and impact of working in public safety roles.

Leverage Social Media Platforms: Utilize social media platforms such as Facebook, Twitter, LinkedIn, and Instagram to promote your recruitment efforts and engage with potential candidates. Share engaging content, behind-the-scenes glimpses of agency life, and success stories to humanize your brand and attract candidates.

Optimize Search Engine Visibility: Enhance your agency's visibility on search engines by optimizing your website and recruitment content for relevant keywords and phrases. Use search engine optimization (SEO) techniques to improve your website's ranking in search results and increase organic traffic from potential candidates.

Implement Data Analytics Tools: Implement data analytics tools such as Google Analytics, Facebook Insights, and LinkedIn Analytics to track and measure the performance of your recruitment campaigns. Monitor key metrics such as website traffic, engagement rates, and conversion rates to assess the effectiveness of your digital marketing efforts.

Overcoming Challenges and Roadblocks

<u>Resistance to Change:</u> Overcoming resistance to change within public safety agencies may be a challenge when introducing digital marketing tactics. Educate stakeholders about the benefits of digital marketing in recruitment, provide training and support, and demonstrate the ROI of implementing digital strategies.

<u>Limited Resources:</u> Public safety agencies may face resource constraints, including budgetary limitations and staffing shortages when implementing digital marketing tactics. Prioritize high-impact initiatives, leverage free or low-cost marketing tools and platforms, and explore partnerships with external stakeholders to maximize resources and achieve recruitment goals.

<u>Compliance and Regulation:</u> Public safety agencies must navigate compliance and regulatory requirements when implementing digital marketing tactics, particularly regarding data privacy and security. Ensure compliance with relevant laws and regulations such as the General Data Protection Regulation (GDPR) and the Health Insurance Portability and Accountability Act (HIPAA) to protect candidate information and mitigate legal risks.

Embracing digital marketing tactics is essential for public safety agencies seeking to enhance their recruitment efforts and attract top talent in today's competitive landscape. By leveraging targeted messaging, social media platforms, search engine optimization, and data analytics, agencies can increase brand visibility, engage with potential candidates, and achieve better recruitment outcomes. Through strategic implementation, overcoming challenges, and continuous optimization, public safety agencies can leverage the power of digital marketing to build strong, resilient teams.

CHAPTER 17:
THE FUTURE OF POLICE AND FIRE RECRUITING IN THE DIGITAL AGE

As we venture further into the digital age, the landscape of police and fire recruiting is undergoing a profound transformation. With advancements in technology, changes in demographics, and shifts in candidate expectations, the future of recruiting in public safety agencies is poised to be dynamic and innovative. In this chapter, we will explore the emerging trends, challenges, and opportunities shaping the future of police and fire recruiting in the digital age.

Technology Integration in Recruitment

Artificial Intelligence and Automation: The integration of artificial intelligence (AI) and automation will revolutionize police and fire recruiting processes. AI-powered chatbots will handle initial candidate inquiries, screening, and scheduling, streamlining communication and enhancing efficiency. Automation tools will streamline administrative tasks, allowing recruiters to focus on building relationships with candidates.

Virtual Recruitment Events: Virtual recruitment events will become increasingly prevalent, allowing public safety agencies to reach candidates regardless of geographical location. Virtual job fairs, online information sessions, and interactive webinars will provide opportunities for candidates to learn about career opportunities and engage with recruiters from the comfort of their own homes.

Augmented Reality (AR) and Virtual Reality (VR): AR and VR technologies will transform the recruitment experience, providing candidates with immersive simulations of police and fire training scenarios. VR-based assessment tools will allow candidates to demonstrate their skills and abilities in realistic virtual environments, providing recruiters with valuable insights into their suitability for the role.

Data-Driven Recruitment Strategies

Predictive Analytics: Public safety agencies will leverage predictive analytics to anticipate future recruitment needs, identify high-potential candidates, and tailor recruitment strategies accordingly. By analyzing historical data and trends, agencies can make informed decisions about resource allocation, candidate sourcing, and outreach efforts.

Personalized Marketing Campaigns: Data-driven marketing campaigns will enable public safety agencies to personalize their messaging and content to resonate with specific candidate demographics and preferences. By leveraging data analytics, agencies can identify the most effective channels, messages, and tactics for reaching and engaging their target audience.

Continuous Performance Monitoring: Real-time monitoring of recruitment metrics will allow agencies to track the effectiveness of their strategies and make adjustments as needed. Key performance indicators (KPIs) such as applicant conversion rates, time-to-fill, and retention rates will provide valuable insights into the success of recruitment initiatives and areas for improvement.

Diversity and Inclusion Initiatives

<u>Targeted Outreach Programs:</u> Public safety agencies will implement targeted outreach programs to attract candidates from underrepresented communities, including women and minorities. Collaborations with community organizations, schools, and advocacy groups will help agencies build relationships and foster trust within diverse communities.

<u>Implicit Bias Training:</u> Training programs on implicit bias and cultural competency will become standard practice for recruiters and hiring managers in public safety agencies. By raising awareness of unconscious biases and promoting inclusive hiring practices, agencies can create more diverse and inclusive workforces that reflect the communities they serve.

<u>Mentorship and Support Networks:</u> Mentorship and support networks for minority candidates and employees will play a crucial role in retention and career advancement. Establishing mentorship programs, affinity groups, and leadership development initiatives will provide opportunities for professional growth and support for underrepresented individuals in public safety careers.

Ethical and Transparent Recruitment Practices

<u>Transparency and Accountability:</u> Public safety agencies will prioritize transparency and accountability in recruitment

processes to build trust with candidates and the community. Clear communication, consistent messaging, and ethical behavior will be paramount in attracting and retaining top talent while upholding the integrity of the recruitment process.

Ethical Use of Data: Agencies will adhere to strict ethical guidelines and data privacy regulations when collecting and analyzing candidate information. Protecting candidate privacy and maintaining the security of sensitive data will be essential to preserve trust and credibility in recruitment practices.

Community Engagement and Feedback: Public safety agencies will actively engage with the community to solicit feedback on recruitment practices and priorities. Community input will inform recruitment strategies, outreach efforts, and diversity initiatives, ensuring that agencies remain responsive to the needs and expectations of the communities they serve.

The future of police and fire recruiting in the digital age promises to be dynamic, innovative, and inclusive. By embracing emerging technologies, leveraging data-driven strategies, and prioritizing diversity and inclusion, public safety agencies can attract and retain a diverse workforce capable of meeting the evolving needs of their communities. Through ethical and transparent recruitment practices, agencies can build trust with candidates and stakeholders while upholding the integrity and professionalism of the public safety profession.

ABOUT THE AUTHOR

Christopher Smith

Christopher is a 20+ year fire service veteran who serves as a public information officer with a large fire department in the metro Atlanta area.

Christopher and his wife have also owned a large digital marketing company for 20+ years.

These two worlds combine to provide the expertise and experience to implement digital recruiting techniques that reach Gen Z and Millenial candidates.

Christopher holds a bachelor's degree in public safety leadership from Reinhardt University in Waleska, GA, and a master's of education in adult education from Colorado State University in Fort Collins, CO.

You can reach Christopher via his email at: cs@firerecruiting.co

www.ingramcontent.com/pod-product-compliance
Lightning Source LLC
Chambersburg PA
CBHW072247310526
45795CB00011B/297